It's
Delicious!

Food for Family and Friends from

HOSPITAL HOSPITALITY HOUSE

The Dietz Press
Richmond, Virginia
2003

Cover design by Charles Ryan Associates

Text Design by Susan Mark Huie

Copyright 2003
Hospital Hospitality House of Richmond, Inc.

Published by
The Dietz Press
Richmond, Virginia

Printed in the United States of America

ISBN# 0-87517-119-2

Library of Congress Control Number 2003090964

The Hospital Hospitality House Story

A loved one in the hospital, debilitating outpatient treatments, lengthy rehabilitation. These are the emotionally and physically exhausting circumstances that many people face every day. Now add the burden of having to cope with these traumatic medical and additional financial stresses when treatment is in a distant city, far from the comforts and supports of home. Enter Richmond's Hospital Hospitality House, a haven where outpatients, caretakers and family members can receive room, board and vital support.

Once a failing hotel, worn and tattered, the Hospital Hospitality House is now a thoughtfully renovated 121-room facility designed to meet the special needs of its guests. Thanks to the generous donors and volunteers, HHH offers everything from washers, dryers, and microwaves to televisions, bingo night, and exercise equipment. Books and tapes fill the library shelves. A stocked pantry and walk-in refrigerator and freezer complement four well-equipped kitchens. But more than that, the Hospital Hospitality House is people. A friendly smile, a listening ear, a hand to hold. To those in medical crisis, it is a place to call home.

This is what former HHH guests have to say about the Hospital Hospitality House.

"We want to thank you all so much for all the kindness shown to us during our stay. I really don't know what we would have done if it were not for the service you offer. We will never forget the many friends we met while staying there."

"Thank you so much for giving us such a secure haven when things around us seemed so frightening. My parents are older and your lovely room, your coffee, and especially your shuttle service were a God sent. My brother is home and well now and we are so thankful - but we will never forget you and your wonderful people. You could feel God's presence everywhere."

"The family spoke very highly of you for the care given when their loved one was so ill. It's so nice to know that there are caring, compassionate people to help in these terrible times when a loved one is sick and tragically terminal."

"Thank you for all you did to make my brother's last days as comfortable as possible."

"Due to a tragic accident, our mother was hospitalized at MCVH for much of December and January. Our out-of-town family members' use of the Hospitality House met our need for a pleasant and caring place to stay near the hospital during a very difficult and stressful period in our lives. For this we thank you from the bottom of our hearts."

"I will never forget! I was involved in an automobile accident in Northern Virginia and would spend the next two months in MCVH. I would have my life saved but would eventually lose my left arm. Although the medical and personal care that I received was excellent, it was the gift of shelter available to my parents that saved me. My parents, from Western Pennsylvania, would spend each Monday through Friday at my bedside, and return home on weekends. My brother would fill the weekends, my parents returning on Sunday nights. They never could have afforded lodging for such a period of time and I would have struggled without their support. Thank God for the Hospitality House - it was a lifesaver for me. Thank you."

Acknowledgments

We would like to acknowledge and gratefully thank the Cookbook Committee who gave so much of their time, effort and enthusiasm to this fundraising effort:

Babs Jackson, President & CEO
Hospital Hospitality House

Annette Gelber, Committee Chair,
Hospital Hospitality House Volunteer

Tonya Lancaster, Administrative Assistant,
Hospital Hospitality House

Steve Ault, Operations Manager,
Hospital Hospitality House

Linda Ferguson,
Hospital Hospitality House Volunteer

Nancy Powell, Director Corporate Relations,
Universal Leaf Tobacco Co., Inc.

Harriet Frank,
Universal Leaf Tobacco Co., Inc.

Louis Mahoney,
Hospital Hospitality House Volunteer

Karen Schonauer
Hospital Hospitality House Volunteer

With heartfelt thanks, we wish to acknowledge *Charles Ryan Associates* for their valuable assistance towards the development of design, advertising and marketing programs for this, our very first cookbook.

Our deep appreciation of the following group of people who gave of their time, effort and culinary expertise to cull the hundreds of recipes we received from our contributors.

Members of the Circle of Friends

Members of the Richmond Culinary Guild
Barbara Anchell
Sandra Brooks
Annette Gelber
Cathy Hinton
Carol Jarrett

We are honored and delighted that wonderful Richmond Area chefs contributed their recipes to the Celebrity Chef's section of our cookbook:

Chef Russell Cook,
Millie's Restaurant
Chef Michael Palazzotto,
Angela's Ristorante
Chef Nancy Cohen,
Café Mandolin
Chef David Bruce Clarke,
Virginia Gourmet, Chef Instructor
Chef Marcel Desaulniers,
The Trellis Restaurant
Chef John Maxwell,
Chef Maxwell's Kitchen
Chef Paolo Randazzo,
Franco's Restaurant
Chef Josef R. Schelch
The Homestead
The Greenbier
White Sulphur Springs, West Virginia

Last but not least, we owe a very special vote of thanks to all the people who contributed the recipes that have made this project a reality. We could not have done it without you!

Table of Contents

Celebrity Chef Recipes

Saltimbocca

Submitted by Chef Michael Palazzotto
Richmond, Virginia

INGREDIENTS:

8 ounces thinly sliced veal, scallopine cut,
   lightly dredged in flour
4 tablespoons olive oil
2 cloves minced garlic
2 tablespoons Italian chopped parsley

White pepper to taste
8 slices extra thin prosciutto
8 ounces sliced fresh mozzarella
4 ounces sherry

Heat olive oil in large skillet on medium heat. Add dredged veal, brown one minute each side. Add minced garlic, parsley and white pepper to taste, sauté 2 minutes. Add prosciutto and sherry. Reduce heat and simmer 2–3 minutes. Divide into 2 oven-safe plates, top with sliced fresh mozzarella cheese. Broil in oven until lightly golden. Garnish with parsley.

SERVES: 2

Born and raised in Palermo, Sicily, Chef Michael knew as a young boy that he was fascinated by the art of cooking. He attended Albeghera School of Culinary Arts, where he specialized in Southern Italian cuisine. Chef Michael followed his dream of coming to the United States where he settled in New York and worked as a sous chef at Villa Borghese. In 1984, Chef Michael and his wife Denise opened Angela's Ristorante in Richmond, Virginia. The restaurant is named after his mother. They are successfully beginning their nineteenth year in business and look forward to serving those delicious meals for many more years.

Braised Osso Buco with Root Vegetable Ragout

Submitted by Millie's and Executive Chef Russell Cook
Richmond, Virginia

INGREDIENTS:

2 medium carrots, ¾" dice
2 parsnips, ¾" dice
2 medium turnips and/or salsify, ¾" dice
¼ cup olive oil
2 to 4 osso buco (veal shank cut across the bone, 1½ to 2" thick) can substitute lamb shank, short ribs, oxtails — any good braising meat

4 peeled garlic cloves
4 to 6 boiling onions
A few sprigs of thyme and rosemary, roughly chopped
Salt and pepper
1½ cups white wine
1½ cups veal or beef stock
1½ cups chicken stock

NEED: One roasting pan with sides high enough to accommodate all ingredients and tight fitting lid or aluminum foil.

Cut carrots, parsnips and turnips into ¾" dice. Heat olive oil in roasting pan directly on large burner at medium to medium-high heat. Sear osso buco, moving occasionally, until they begin to brown. Add garlic, onions and chopped vegetables, stirring periodically to avoid burning. Add herbs, salt and pepper. Sauté for approximately 5 minutes or until the vegetables start to get a bit of color. Turn the osso buco over and carefully add the wine. Allow the wine to come to a simmer, then add the veal and chicken stock. Cover with lid or foil and place in a 300° F oven for 2 to 2½ hours or until the meat is falling off the bone.

SERVES: 2–4

Thai-Style Spicy Shrimp with Asparagus, Shiitakes, Red Cabbage and Fettucine (or Rice Noodles)

Submitted by Millie's and Executive Chef Russell Cook
Richmond, Virginia

INGREDIENTS:

¼ cup peanut oil

42 large shrimp, shelled, tails on, deveined

1 tablespoon Thai chili sauce (sambal olek)

1½ teaspoons minced garlic

1 cup sliced shiitake mushrooms

1 cup shredded red cabbage

1 cup fresh asparagus, sliced on bias into
    1½" pieces

1 cup white wine

1 tablespoon sugar

2½ tablespoons Worcestershire sauce

2½ tablespoons fish sauce (nam prik)

1½ pounds fettucine or rice noodles,
    cooked and drained

6 lime wedges, more to taste

Chopped peanuts

Cilantro to taste

In a wok or large skillet, heat oil until smoking and add shrimp, chili sauce and garlic. Sauté until shrimp turn pink and are almost cooked. Transfer shrimp to a bowl, reserving the oil in the pan. Add shiitakes, cabbage and asparagus to pan and deglaze with the white wine. (To deglaze, simply add the wine to the pan juices to release the flavorful bits in the bottom of the pan). Add sugar, Worcestershire and fish sauces. Cook vegetables in mixture for about 4 to 5 minutes until cooked but firm. Add pasta to vegetables and add oil and juices from reserved shrimp. Toss to heat thoroughly. Divide among 6 pasta bowls and keep warm. Return pan to medium heat, add shrimp (toss in pan juices that remain) to heat and finish cooking. Sauté approximately one minute and when done, divide shrimp among pasta bowls. Squeeze a lime wedge over each bowl of pasta, sprinkle with chopped peanuts and garnish with fresh cilantro.

SERVES: 6

Since opening in 1989, Millie's has been garnering rave reviews for its cutting edge approach to food and vintage ambience. Millie's changes its dinner menu every three weeks—focusing on the freshest possible ingredients, innovative preparation and artful presentation. Numerous national publications have positively reviewed Millie's over the years, including *Southern Living*, "stand in line if you must"; *Bon Appetit*, "Millie's . . . the best symbol of an updated Richmond" and the *Los Angeles Times*, "Millie's is truly a gem — fun, fresh and forward-thinking." Millie's complements its innovative menu with an extensive international wine and beer list, featuring eclectic and lesser known wine varietals.

Executive Chef Russell Cook is a self-taught chef, who worked his way up through the ranks at Millie's. He served as sous chef for 4 years and was promoted to executive in July of 2000. Although Chef Cook is interested in all styles of cooking, he is particularly fond of Asian and Indonesian styles and ingredients.

Banana Chocolate Chip Cake

Submitted by Nancy Cohen
Richmond, Virginia

INGREDIENTS:

½ cup vegan margarine (without whey)
1 cup sugar
1 tablespoon "egg replacer," mixed in 2
    tablespoons water
½ cup soy milk
2½ cups flour

2 large overripe bananas
1 teaspoon baking powder
1 teaspoon baking soda
1 tablespoon vanilla extract
1 cup chocolate chips

In electric mixer bowl, cream together margarine and sugar until fluffy. Add egg replacer and soy milk and stir until blended. With mixer off, add flour, baking powder and baking soda. Beat at medium speed until well-blended. Add vanilla extract and bananas (cut in chunks). Mix at low/medium speed until bananas are well incorporated into batter. Stir in chocolate chips. Bake in greased bundt pan at 375° F for 45 minutes. Cool; sprinkle with confectioner's sugar.

SERVES: 12

Nancy Cohen is the owner & chef at Cafe Mandolin.

Chesapeake Bay Crab Soup

Submitted by D. Bruce Clarke

INGREDIENTS:

½ dozen crabs (live or fresh frozen)
1–1½ quarts water to cover
2 or 3 chicken necks or backs (optional)
1 cup carrots, small dice
1 cup celery, small dice
½ cup onion, small dice
4 slices of bacon, (frozen and
    chopped fine)

4 tablespoons all purpose flour
1 bay leaf
2 cups frozen mixed vegetables
    (without peas)
1½ cups chopped and peeled tomatoes
Old Bay Seasoning to taste (optional)
8 ounces fresh crabmeat
Salt and pepper to taste

Remove carapace from crab, (pointy outer shell) remove dead-man (lungs) rinse lightly (take care not to wash mustard from shell), chop crab in half, then chop each leg section along the dividing cartilage (back fin etc.) Cover with fresh cold tap water, add chicken parts if using. Bring to a boil, reduce heat and simmer 35–40 minutes. Using slotted spoon, remove *scum and discard* as needed.

While making crab stock, render bacon and smother carrot, onion and celery, when onions are clear and carrots are tender add flour to make roux, allow roux to cook 3 to 5 minutes while stirring so as not to scorch. (burnt flavor) Strain crab stock into vegetable and roux mixture, *discard chicken* and reserve crab sections.

Add tomatoes, mixed vegetables and bay leaf, bring to a second boil, reduce heat and simmer for 20 minutes or until frozen vegetables are tender, add crab and crab parts, Old Bay and adjust seasonings.

SERVES: 4–6

David Bruce Clarke
Chef Instructor, Virginia Gourmet
Member, American Culinary Federation (ACF) since 1976
Member ACF, Virginia Chefs Association since 1989
ACF Virginia Chefs Association's "Chapter Chef of the Year" 1997
Lead Chef Instructor, J. Sargeant Reynolds Community College
Executive Chef, Jefferson Lakeside Country Club
Banquet Chef, Country Club of Virginia
Executive Chef, Angelina's Restaurant, Baltimore, Maryland
Secretary, ACF, Baltimore Chef's Association

Sous Chef, Baltimore Country Club, Baltimore, Maryland
Sous Chef, Suburban Country Club, Baltimore, Maryland
Chef Instructor, Baltimore's International Culinary Arts Institute
Graduate Baltimore International Culinary Arts Institute, 1975
Honor Graduate, U.S. Army Quarter Masters School, Cook's and Baker's, 1968

Grilled Pork Loin Medallions with Thinly Sliced Country Ham and Pecan-Studded Jasmine Rice

Submitted by The Trellis Restaurant
Marcel Desaulniers, Executive Chef
Williamsburg, Virginia

INGREDIENTS:

2 tablespoons unsalted butter
½ cup yellow onion, minced
Salt and white pepper to taste
1 cup Jasmine Rice
1¾ cups chicken stock

1½ pounds Lean Generation Pork
    Tenderloin, trimmed of fat and silver
    skin, cut into 1½ ounce pieces and
    lightly pounded ¼ inch thick
4 ea. ⅛ inch thick slices Country Ham

GARNISH

1 cup toasted Pecan halves
½ pound fresh watercress, trimmed,
    washed, and dried
1 tablespoon carrot, peeled, ends removed,
    and diced into ¹⁄₁₆ inch pieces
1 tablespoon red bell pepper, washed,
    seeded, pith and seeds removed,
    and diced into ¹⁄₁₆ inch pieces

1 tablespoon yellow squash, washed,
    ends removed, and yellow part only
    diced into ¹⁄₁₆ inch pieces
1 tablespoon zucchini, washed, ends
    removed, and green part only diced
    into ¹⁄₁₆ inch pieces

MAKE THE JASMINE RICE

Heat 2 tablespoons butter in a medium saucepan over medium-high heat. When hot, add the ½ cup yellow onion. Season with salt and white pepper, and sauté for 2 minutes, until tender. Add the jasmine rice and stir to coat with the butter and onions. Add the hot chicken stock and stir to blend. Bring to a boil. Cover the saucepan and reduce the heat to medium and continue to cook the rice until tender, about 15 minutes. Remove the rice from the heat. Adjust the seasoning with salt and freshly ground black pepper. Set the rice aside to keep warm.

GRILL THE PORK & SERVE

Season the pork medallions with salt and black pepper. Quickly grill the medallions over a medium hot fire on both sides, being sure not to over cook.

Evenly divide the jasmine rice between the four plates. Fashion a cornucopia out of the sliced country ham and place it in the center of the rice facing up. Fill these "hamucopias" with some of the watercress. Place 4 pieces of the grilled pork on top of the rice for each portion. Finally stud the rice with the toasted pecans and sprinkle each plate with some of the ¹⁄₁₆ inch diced vegetables. Serve immediately.

SERVES: 4

Marcel Desaulniers is the executive chef and owner of the Trellis Restaurant in Williamsburg, Virginia. A 1965 graduate of the Culinary Institute of America, Marcel has received several national awards, including *Food and Wine* magazine's Honor Roll of American Chefs, Who's Who of Food & Beverage in America, the prestigious Ivy Award from *Restaurants and Institutions*, the 1993 James Beard Award for Best Chef Mid-Atlantic States, the highly coveted Silver Plate award from the International Foodservice Manufacturers Association, and in 1999 the James Beard Award for Outstanding Pastry Chef in America.

State Fair Chili
Submitted by Chef John Maxwell

This recipe won the Virginia State Fair Chili Competition in 1997

INGREDIENTS:

1 tablespoon garlic oil
8 ounces onions, chopped
2 pounds beef, cubed
1 pound pork, cubed
1 cup green pepper, diced
2 tablespoons minced garlic
1 cup salsa
½ cup tomato paste
½ cup red wine
2 bay leaves
4 tablespoons cumin

2 chipotle chiles, minced
2 tablespoons tamari, San J tamari sauce
2 ancho chili peppers, minced
1 cup strong coffee
½ gallon beef stock
2 cups black beans, cooked or canned
2 cups red beans, cooked or canned
1 gallon tomatoes, diced
2 tablespoons oregano
¼ cup vinegar, malt

Heat the oil in a stock pot. Brown the beef and the pork. Add the onions, and garlic and sauté until the garlic is browned. Add the tomato paste and cook for 5 minutes. Deglaze with red wine and add the tamari. Add the remaining ingredients and cook for about 1 hour.

SERVES: 24

Crab and Smithfield Ham Quiche

Submitted by Chef John Maxwell

INGREDIENTS:

¾ cup mayonnaise
3 tablespoons flour
4 eggs, beaten
1¾ cups heavy cream
¼ cup celery, diced
¼ cup red bell peppers, finely diced

1 tablespoon minced garlic
1 pound crabmeat
1 cup Smithfield ham, shredded
12 ounces smoked Gouda, grated
1 tablespoon Old Bay seasoning
Salt and pepper, to taste

Sauté the celery, bell pepper and garlic in 1 tablespoon of butter. Combine the mayonnaise, flour, eggs, and cream, mixing well. Add the sauteed vegetables and the Smithfield ham. Season with Old Bay, salt, and pepper. Fold in the crabmeat, gently. Divide the mixture between the two pie shells and bake at 350° F in a still oven for one hour and 10 minutes. Allow the quiche to sit for 10 minutes before cutting. May be reheated in a microwave at medium power for 2 minutes.

SERVES: 8

East Virginia Crabcakes

Submitted by Chef John Maxwell

INGREDIENTS:

⅓ cup mayonnaise
1 tablespoon Dijon mustard
1 dash Lea & Perrins Worcestershire sauce
1 tablespoon lemon juice
1 teaspoon Old Bay seasoning
¼ cup minced shallots

1 tablespoon minced chives
1 slice white bread, crumbed,
    crust removed
1 dash Tobasco Sauce
1 whole egg
1 pound crab, jumbo lump

Mix all wet ingredients together. Fold in bread crumbs, onions, and chives. Very gently pick the crabmeat free of shell without breaking up the lumps. Very carefully fold the crab into the mixture.

SERVES: 3

Sally Lunn Bread

Submitted by Chef John Maxwell

INGREDIENTS:

8 cups bread flour
1 cup milk
1 cup water
¼ pound butter

⅔ cup sugar
¼ cup yeast
2 tablespoons salt
6 eggs

In a saucepan combine the milk, water and butter and heat until the butter just melts. In a mixing bowl, combine half the flour, the yeast, salt and sugar. Add the warm liquid and mix well. Add the eggs, two at a time adding flour between each pair of eggs. Mix the eggs in well and quickly to prevent the hot batter from cooking the eggs. Make sure the eggs are well incorporated before adding more flour. The dough should form a smooth ball, not as firm as traditional bread, but still firm enough to hold its shape well. Lightly oil a clean bowl and place the dough in it. Lightly oil the surface of the dough and cover the bowl with plastic wrap. Place the dough in a warm, dark place to rise until double in size. Liberally grease (butter) two bundt type pans. Wherever there is no grease, the batter will stick. Divide the risen dough equally between the two pans and return to rise until double in size again. When fully risen the second time, transfer the pans of dough to a preheated 360° F oven and bake until very rich brown (about 20 minutes).

This bread is exceptional as a base for other foods such as eggs, creamed mushrooms, seafood and the like, as well as for toast. It also makes a wonderful dinner bread and may be risen and baked in popover form.

SERVES: 10

Chef John Maxwell has been a fixture in the Richmond food scene since 1976 when he and his father opened Maxwell's Restaurant in the city's West End. Since that time, the chef has been active as a caterer, restaurateur and television personality.

His television program, Chef Maxwell's Kitchen aired in the Richmond area on what is now the Rich TV network. Beginning in January 2002, the chef has joined forces with the Virginia Farm Bureau and Virginia's Finest, a division of the Virginia Department of Agriculture to present Chef Maxwell's Kitchen as a segment on "Down Home Virginia," a program with state wide distribution.

Chef Maxwell has a reputation for civic and charitable involvement having served on the board of directors for "Chef and the Child" a national hunger and nutrition organization of the American Culinary Federation. The chef has served as board member for the Central Virginia Food Bank, director of Richmond's Community Kitchen and as the provider of summer foodservice for Camp Baker in Chesterfield, a program of the Richmond Area Association for Retarded Persons.

Chef Maxwell serves on the advisory committee of the Hospitality Division of J. Sargent Reynolds Community College and was the chairman of that committee for two years. He currently serves the college as adjunct instructor for the PAVE program which prepares special needs students for careers in professional kitchens. Maxwell is on the advisory committee for New Kent High School's Culinary program and for the Hermitage High School Culinary program. Chef Maxwell serves on the statewide committee for Career and Technical programs for the Virginia Department of Education.

Maxwell's current business interests lay in Magnolia's, a Shop of Southern Specialties. This retail shop in Sandston, Virginia focuses on foods of Virginia and the Southeast United States. The shop houses a teaching kitchen for culinary classes aimed at the nonprofessional and is the location of Chef Maxwell's Catering, one of the region's premier caterers.

Chef Maxwell's national reputation for excellence and for innovation has made him a frequent presenter at conventions, seminars and conferences throughout the United States. The chef has presented demonstrations at the National Restaurant Convention in Chicago, at the American Culinary Federation National Convention on a number of occasions, at the Washington DC International Wine Festival and many others.

Chef Maxwell is the current president of the ACF Virginia Chef's Association. He received the coveted "Certified Executive Chef" (CEC) designation from the American Culinary Federation, and was recently inducted into the prestigious American Academy of Chefs.

Among his many awards, Chef Maxwell has been awarded the Virginia Governor's Cup for Seafood Excellence, two ACF Presidential Medallions, the Louis B. Szathmary Chef Humanitarian Award, numerous local and national competition medals, and is a Maitre Rotisseur of The Chaine des Rotisseurs.

Five-Onion Soup with Crispy Shallots and Fresh Olives

Submitted by The Greenbrier
White Sulphur Springs, West Virginia

INGREDIENTS:

2 tablespoons unsalted butter
4 medium shallots (4 ounces) roughly chopped
1 medium leek, white part only (4 ounces), roughly chopped
1 medium red onion (8 ounces), roughly chopped
2 medium yellow onions, (1 pound), roughly chopped

1 bunch green onions, white part only, roughly chopped
2 quarts chicken stock, preferably homemade
1½ cups heavy cream
Salt and freshly ground black pepper, to taste

In a large heavy-bottomed saucepan, melt the butter and add the shallots, leek and all the onions. Cover and cook over low heat, stirring frequently to prevent burning, until the onions are soft and have turned deep golden brown, 20–30 minutes. Add the chicken stock and simmer uncovered until the onions are very soft, about another 20 minutes. Transfer the soup to a blender and blend until very smooth (do this in batches if necessary). Return the soup to a clean pan, add the cream and bring to a boil. (Simmer the soup a few minutes to thicken slightly, if necessary.) Season with salt and pepper to taste.

GARNISH:

2 shallots, cut in half lengthwise and sliced as thinly as possible
1 teaspoon all-purpose flour

Oil (such as canola, soy or safflower), for deep-frying
1 tablespoon minced fresh chives

To make the shallot garnish: sprinkle the sliced shallots with the flour then toss in a fine strainer to thoroughly coat the shallots and shake off excess flour. Fill a saucepan no more than ⅓ full with oil. Heat the oil to 375° F (if not using a thermometer, fry a few test pieces first). Carefully drop the shallots in the oil and fry, stirring to prevent sticking. The shallots should cook slowly getting light brown after about 45 seconds. When golden brown (no darker than a brown paper bag) remove from the oil with a slotted spoon and drain on paper towels. The garnish may be made up to 8 hours ahead and stored in an airtight container. To serve, ladle the hot soup into warm bowls and top with a spoonful of crispy shallots and a pinch of fresh chives.

SERVES: 8

Sicilian Chicken or Steak

Submitted by Chef Paolo Randazzo
Franco's Restaurant

INGREDIENTS:

4 thin rib-eye steaks or chicken breasts (pounded thinly)
2 cups bread crumbs
¼ cup chopped parsley
½ cup finely chopped fresh garlic
2 cups chopped fresh basil
2 cups extra virgin olive oil
2 lemons
4 large Portobello mushrooms

2 large Fresh Mozzarella balls sliced in to ½ inch slices
Balsamic vinegar
1 large bunch arugula or enough for a salad
3 chopped tomatoes
Six Pack of Beer of your choice
1 Bottle Pinot Grigio
3 large serving platters

Start your grill, set at High heat.

Drink a beer during preparation.

FOR THE SICILIAN STEAKS OR CHICKEN BREAST: In a large flat plate mix bread crumbs, ¼ cup garlic, parsley, salt and pepper to taste. In a large flat plate pour 1 cup olive oil and coat steaks or breasts well then coat with seasoned bread crumbs. Set aside.

FOR THE PORTOBELLO MUSHROOMS: Coat the mushrooms with olive oil and rub with garlic. Set aside. Place mozzarella slices on a serving platter.

FOR THE SALAD: Clean arugula in a water bath twice and drain and dry well. Add 1 cup fresh basil and top with chopped tomatoes. Set aside.

FOR THE BREAD: Slice bread about ¾ inch thick and brush with olive oil. Set aside.

FOR THE GRILLING: Drink a beer while grilling.

Take to the grill prepared meats, mushrooms, bread, 2 large serving platters and the prepared mozzarella slices. Brush the grill rack with a little olive oil and place the Portobellos and bread on the rack. Grill mushrooms until fork tender and bread until golden and with seared grill marks. Place mushrooms on top of the fresh mozzarella cheese slices. Divide with olive oil, balsamic vinegar, salt and pepper. Top with fresh basil. If grilling room allows place a piece of aluminum foil on top the grill rack large enough to accommodate the prepared meats. Let the foil get hot then brush it with olive oil. Place prepared meats a top the foil and grill to your liking. Season arugula with olive oil, lemon, salt and pepper.

Pour the wine and enjoy your dinner.

Executive Chef Randazzo was born and raised in Palermo, an area rich with tradition and a distinct culinary background. He studied in Italy under renowned Chef Antonio Pirozzollo, working in Italy, New York and Florida before opening Franco's Ristorante with his wife Rhonda in 1987.

Executive Chef Randazzo takes as his mission, an effort to modernize Richmond's concepts about *Cucina Italiana* by blending interpretations that are contemporary in Italy with a classical process while using quality ingredients. The restaurant features in its changing seasonal menu the latest movements in Italian cooking, as well as dishes built around the freshest seasonal ingredients available.

(Awards) Critics List 1988–2001, *Four Stars, Style Magazine*
Best Italian Restaurant, *Richmond Magazine*
Best Restaurant in Henrico, *Richmond Magazine*
Best Italian Restaurant, *Citysearch Audience and Critics Choice Winners 2000, 2001, 2002*
Best Restaurant in Henrico, *Richmond Magazine*

Macadamia Nut Crusted Breast of Chicken, Lemon Sauce

Submitted by The Homestead
Josef R. Schelch, Executive Chef

INGREDIENTS:

1 tablespoon diced shallots
½ cup diced shiitake mushrooms
1 cup fine diced mushrooms
1 tablespoon diced sun dried tomatoes
3 tablespoons diced red peppers
1 teaspoon chopped fresh thyme
1 cup cooked Uncle Ben's rice (please not
  minute rice)

1 cup cooked wild rice (optional)
1 teaspoon chopped garlic
4 tablespoons (white) bread crumbs
½ cup shredded mozzarella
2 cups heavy (whipping) cream
½ cup white wine
1 tablespoon olive oil
30-baby spinach leaves

FOR THE FILLING:

OPTIONAL: When ready to use filling add if desired 3–4 ounces lump crabmeat (pick crabmeat over for shells) or fine diced cooked shrimp.

Reduce 2 cups of heavy cream in a stainless steel saucepan (Calphalon pot will do) over medium heat to 1 cup.

In a stainless steel sauce pan (Calphalon is acceptable) over medium to high heat, add olive oil, mushrooms, shiitake mushrooms, garlic, shallots and red peppers and sauté for 5 minutes while stirring occasionally, then add thyme and sun-dried tomatoes, keep cooking for a couple minutes before adding both rice, blend well and simmer on medium heat, adding white wine and reduced cream, blend well and simmer to a thick consistency while stirring, add spinach and take off the heat. Let cool some before adding mozzarella.

When stuffing is cool, cover with Saran Wrap and refrigerate. (This can be 24 hours ahead.)

FOR THE CHICKEN ROULADES:

5 boneless and skinless breast of chicken
  (8–10 ounces each)
Salt, ground white pepper
1 cup flour
3 eggs well beaten

2 cups breadcrumbs (Japanese if
  available)
1 cup fine chopped macadamia nuts
1 cup peanut oil

Butterfly chicken breasts, place each on plastic wrap, cover chicken with a second piece of wrap, lightly pound chicken with a meat mallet or bottom of a small fry (omelette) pan evenly to approx. ¼ inch thickness. Refrigerate chicken until ready to use wrapped.

TO BREAD AND COOK THE ROULADES: Remove top of plastic wrap and add approx. ½–¾ cup of filling *in the center of chicken*, spread to the width of chicken. With the help of plastic, roll and overlap chicken around stuffing to a sausage like appearance. Keep covered in refrigerator and 15 minutes before use place in freezer for 5 minutes for easier handling.

In 3 soup plates or pie pans in separate dishes, put flour with pinch of salt, and pepper, eggs and breadcrumbs mixed with macadamia nuts.

Remove all plastic from roulades. Coat chicken (one by one) in the flour, then egg-wash, let excess egg drip off and last roll gently in breadcrumb mixture, patting crumbs to the chicken.

Set oven at 350° F. Using a sauté pan (heavy bottom pan) or cast iron skillet over medium to high heat, add ¾ cup peanut oil, when hot add chicken roulades and brown evenly on all sides using tongs or spatula to turn. Remove from skillet to a sheet pan (cookie pan) or metal pie pan. When ready to serve allow 14 minutes. Put in preheated oven for 3 minutes, reduce heat to 325° F and bake 6 more minutes, let rest roulades rest in a warm (not hot) place for 5 minutes before slicing each roll in 4–6 slices. Add sauce around not over or under chicken slices. Sprinkle some cut chives or chopped parsley.

LEMON SAUCE:

Reduce ½ cup white wine with 1 teaspoon chopped shallots to half,

Add ½ cup fresh squeezed lemon juice

½ teaspoon fine diced or grated lemon peel (yellow skin only)

Bring to a simmer, whip in ½ cup heavy cream and simmer while stirring to a creamy consistency.

Season with salt and pepper

SERVES: 7–8

"Homestead" Virginia Apple Soup

Submitted by The Homestead

INGREDIENTS:

2 cups apple juice
2 cups white wine
½ stick cinnamon
1½ tablespoons minute tapioca

1 cup peeled and fine diced apples
1 tablespoon calvados
2 teaspoons sugar (optional)
2 tablespoons sour cream

Bring apple juice, white wine and cinnamon stick to boil, add tapioca, blend well with whip and simmer for 10 minutes. Add diced apples and remove from heat. Let soup cool, remove cinnamon stick, refrigerate. Before serving add calvados and whip in sour cream. If soup is too thick, add apple juice. Served chilled. Garnish with fresh mint leaves.

SERVES: 4

"Homestead" Scones

Submitted by The Homestead

INGREDIENTS:

2½ cups flour
1 tablespoon baking powder
½ teaspoon salt
¼ pound butter

½ cup sugar
⅔ cup heavy cream (a little more is
generally needed)

Mix dry ingredients with butter until sandy mixture. Add cream; mix until forms soft dough. Cut ½ inch thick scones. Bake at 350° F for 12–15 minutes. Brush with sour cream. Serve with jelly and preserves.

"Homestead" Muffins

Submitted by The Homestead

INGREDIENTS:

IN LARGE BOWL SIFT:

4 cups bread flour

2¼ cups sugar

4 teaspoons baking soda

4 teaspoons cinnamon flavoring

½ teaspoon salt

STIR IN:

4 cups grated carrots

1 cup raisins

1 cup chopped pecans

1 cup coconut

2 apples cored and grated

IN MIXING BOWL:

Add 6 eggs

2 cups peanut oil

4 teaspoons vanilla flavoring

Stir in flour mixture until combined. Spoon into greased muffin pans. Bake at 350°F for approximately 15–20 minutes.

YIELDS: 3 dozen

Appetizers and Beverages

Mini Pineapple Bacon Appetizers   Submitted by Louis Mahoney
Richmond, Virginia

INGREDIENTS:

1 can crushed pineapple, drained
5–6 slices bacon, cooked and crumbled
¾ tablespoon maple syrup
1 teaspoon flour

1 package (15 ounces) refrigerated
   pie crusts
1 egg
1 tablespoon water

Preheat oven to 400° F.

Stir together pineapple, bacon, maple syrup and flour in a small bowl. Set aside. Cut ten 3¾ inch circles from pie crust, using drinking glass or biscuit cutter. Place on cookie sheet sprayed with vegetable cooking spray. Spread 1 tablespoon pineapple filling over each crust. Fold up edges to make a shallow crust around each appetizer, pinching overlapped edges together. Beat egg and water together in a small bowl. Brush edge of crusts with egg wash. Bake at 400° F for 16 to 18 minutes or until crust is golden brown.

SERVES: 10

Adapted from Dole Food Co.

Spinach Dip

Submitted by Meryl Bernstein
Richmond, Virginia

INGREDIENTS:

2 boxes frozen chopped spinach
1 cup mayonnaise
1 cup sour cream (reduced-fat/fine)

1 envelope Hidden Valley Ranch
dressing mix

Cook spinach (either microwave or stovetop) and drain. Squeeze as much liquid out as possible. Mix together with mayonnaise, sour cream and dressing mix. Chill overnight. Next day, re-mix and serve with fresh, cut-up vegetables.

Note: Recipe can be doubled.

SERVES: 12

Spinach Dip

Submitted by Leopal Kirk
Mullen, West Virginia

INGREDIENTS:

1 round loaf of Hawaiian bread
1 10-ounce package frozen chopped
    spinach—thawed)

1 16-ounce sour cream
1 5-ounce can water chestnuts
1 package Ranch dry dressing mix

Squeeze all the water out of thawed spinach. Mix sour cream and dry dressing mix (ranch). Chop water chestnuts fine. Add to sour cream mixture. Cut a round hole in top of bread. Tear the bread that you cut out into small pieces and use it for dipping. Put spinach dip into bread boat when time to serve.

YIELD: Approximately 2 cups dip

Source unknown

Shrimp Dip

Submitted by Nancy Buttermark
Powhatan, Virginia

INGREDIENTS:

1 8-ounce package Monterey Jack
    cheese, shredded
8 ounces shrimp, chopped

1 2¼-ounce can sliced ripe olives, drained
¾ cup mayonnaise
¼ cup chopped green onions

Stir together cheese, shrimp, ripe olives, mayonnaise and green onions in 1-quart microwave-safe dish.

Microwave at high 3 minutes or until cheese melts, stirring after each minute.

Serve with tortilla chips.

YIELDS: ¾ cups

Southern Living Magazine

Shrimp Dip

Submitted by Hazel Cliff (Sunny)
Fredericksburg, Virginia

INGREDIENTS:

2 small packages (3-ounce) cream cheese
2 cans shrimp (5-ounce cans)
1 cup mayonnaise
1 tablespoon capers (optional)

½ lemon, juiced
2 teaspoons onion, grated
1 tablespoon Worcestershire sauce

Mix all ingredients well in blender until you have a fairly smooth paste. Serve with choice of crackers.

YIELDS: approximately 2 to 2½ cups

Friend's recipe

Hot Artichoke Dip

Submitted by Mary Ruth Annerén
Osprey, Florida

INGREDIENTS:

1 small can diced green chilies	1½ cup mayonnaise
1 small jar diced pimentos	4 ounces Monterey Jack cheese
1 14-ounce can artichoke hearts (in water)	½ cup fresh grated Parmesan cheese

Drain chilies, pimentos and artichokes. Chop artichokes into pieces. Combine all ingredients. Place in serving dish. Grate extra Parmesan cheese on top. Bake at 325° F uncovered for 30 minutes. Place under broiler briefly to brown top. Serve with corn chips or crackers.

SERVES: 10

Hot Crab Dip

Submitted by Lesley Greenberg
Richmond, Virginia

INGREDIENTS:

2 sticks butter	¼ can undiluted mushroom soup
2 pounds backfin crab, picked over	Dash Worcestershire sauce
¼ cup white wine	Dash garlic powder

Put all ingredients in large frying pan on low and stir gently just to warm. To serve, place in chafing dish and serve on toast points or crackers.

SERVES: 24 to 36

Source unknown

Ham Spread

Submitted by Vanessa McPherson
Virginia Beach, Virginia

INGREDIENTS:

2 cups cooked cubed ham
1 cup of sour cream

½ teaspoon garlic powder (optional)
Crackers or biscuits

Combine ham, sour cream and garlic powder in blender. Chill for 1 hour. Ready to serve with crackers or biscuits.

SERVES: 15 to 20

Family recipe

Artichoke Spread

Submitted by Sallie Grant
Richmond, Virginia

INGREDIENTS:

1 6-ounce jar marinated artichoke hearts
½ cup Parmesan cheese, grated

⅓ cup mayonnaise
1 large clove garlic, minced

Preheat oven to 350° F. Drain artichoke hearts. Chop artichoke hearts coarsely.

In a mixing bowl, combine artichokes, cheese, mayonnaise and minced garlic. Using a rubber spatula, scrape mixture into ungreased ½-quart baking dish and bake, uncovered, for 20 minutes or until bubbly and slightly browned.

Serve hot, warm or chilled as a spread for crackers or toast rounds.

SERVES: 6 to 8

Family recipe

Crab Dip/Spread

Submitted by Mary Ruth Annerén
Osprey, Florida

INGREDIENTS:

1 pound crabmeat	2 teaspoons Worcestershire
12 ounces cream cheese	½ cup sharp cheddar cheese
1 cup sour cream	1 teaspoon dry mustard
4 tablespoons mayonnaise	2 teaspoons garlic salt
3 teaspoons lemon juice	Milk for consistency

Preheat oven to 325° F.

Blend all ingredients except cheese. Place in casserole. Bake 30–45 minutes. Last 5 minutes, sprinkle cheese over casserole and complete baking. Serve immediately with Triscuits.

SERVES: 15 to 20

Original recipe

Salmon Spread

Submitted by Meryl Bernstein
Richmond, Virginia

INGREDIENTS:

1 15-ounce can salmon	1 teaspoon white horseradish
1 large package Philadelphia cream cheese	½ teaspoon salt
1½ tablespoons lemon juice	¼ teaspoon liquid smoke
2 teaspoons grated onion	

Drain and de-bone salmon, mix together all ingredients and chill overnight. Serve on party rye bread or crackers.

SERVES: 12 to 18

Family recipe

Crabmeat Mousse

Submitted by Jan Urban
Williamsburg, Virginia

INGREDIENTS:

2 3-ounce packages cream cheese
1 small onion, grated
1 can cream of mushroom soup
2 tablespoons Knox gelatin, dissolved in
    1 cup of water

2 6-ounce packages frozen king crab meat
1 cup chopped celery
1 cup mayonnaise

Combine and cook over low heat, cream cheese, onion and soup. Remove from heat, add gelatin. Fold in (picked and shredded) crabmeat, celery and mayonnaise. Pour into large, wet mold. Chill overnight until firm. Unmold and serve on a tray with crackers.

Note: This recipe works well with Imitation crab.

SERVES: approximately 16 to 20

Shrimp Butter

Submitted by Nancy G. Powell
Richmond, Virginia

INGREDIENTS:

½ pound shrimp, cooked and cooled
½ cup butter, room temperature
2 tablespoons green onion, minced
1 teaspoon capers, drained
2 teaspoons fresh lemon juice

½ teaspoon prepared horseradish
¼ teaspoon salt
⅛ teaspoon cayenne pepper
Dash pepper

Put all ingredients in food processor and blend until smooth. Serve on crackers or mini toasts.

SERVES: 6±

Family recipe

Caribbean Appetizer

Submitted by Mrs. Jerry W. Temple
Richmond, Virginia

INGREDIENTS:

2 15-ounce cans of black beans, rinsed
and drained
1 small green bell pepper, chopped
½ cup chopped celery
⅓ cup thinly sliced red onion
1 pound cooked shrimp, cut up into thirds

2 tablespoons chopped cilantro
1½ teaspoons ground cumin
1 clove garlic, minced
7 tablespoons peanut oil
8 tablespoons fresh lime juice
Tabasco and salt to taste

Combine all ingredients and mix well. Refrigerate for several hours. Remove from refrigerator 1 hour before serving. Serve with crackers.

SERVES: 15

Friend's recipe

Caviar Mold

Submitted by Sallie Grant
Richmond, Virginia

INGREDIENTS:

6 hard boiled eggs
1 onion
1 pint sour cream

1 jar caviar (black)
Mayonnaise

Chop eggs finely and put in mixing bowl. Chop onion finely and mix into eggs. Add salt and pepper to taste and enough mayonnaise to bind the eggs and onion together.

Press mixture into oiled mold or shape into a round mound and chill until firm.

Frost mold with sour cream and cover with caviar just before serving. Serve with crackers.

SERVES: 6 to 12 (recipe doubles easily)

Family recipe

Shrimp Party Mold

Submitted by Lesley Greenberg
Richmond, Virginia

INGREDIENTS:

1 lb. shrimp (small & cut up)
1 can tomato soup
¼ cup cold water
1 package unflavored gelatin

8 ounces cream cheese
1 stalk celery, finely chopped
1 cup mayonnaise
Worcestershire sauce to taste

Heat soup until boiling. Dissolve gelatin in cold water. Add to soup mixture.

In separate bowl mix cream cheese, onion, celery, shrimp, mayonnaise and Worcestershire sauce.

Combine all of the above. Pour into lightly oiled "fish" mold and chill over night.

Note: You can use crab instead (1 lb. jumbo lump)

SERVES: 24 to 30 people

Original recipe

Shrimp with Prosciutto

Submitted by Annette Gelber
Richmond, Virginia

INGREDIENTS:

2 tablespoons margarine or butter
2 tablespoons olive or vegetable oil
2 anchovies in oil, finely chopped
1 tablespoon chopped fresh parsley
2 cloves garlic, finely chopped

18 raw jumbo shrimp (in shells)
9 thin slices Prosciutto (or fully cooked
    Virginia Ham) cut in half
½ cup dry white wine
1–2 tablespoons lemon juice

375° F oven. Heat margarine and oil in 9 × 9 × 2 inches baking dish in oven until margarine melts. Mix anchovies, parsley and garlic; spread over mixture in baking dish.

Peel shrimp, leaving tails intact. Make a shallow cut down back of each shrimp and wash out vein. Wrap one-half slice Prosciutto around each shrimp and place on anchovy mixture. Bake uncovered 10 minutes. Pour wine and lemon juice over shrimp. Bake 10 minutes longer—or until shrimp are pink.

SERVES: 18 appetizers

Betty Crocker's New Christmas Cookbook

Cheesy Shrimp Canapes

Submitted by Karen Shea
Richmond, Virginia

INGREDIENTS:

10 slices white bread
2 tablespoons butter
½ teaspoon thyme leaves
6 ounces cooked shrimp, chopped
½ cup shredded Swiss cheese

⅓ cup mayonnaise
½ cup fresh bread crumbs
¼ teaspoon salt (to taste)
Dillweed

Preheat oven to 400° F. Using a 2-inch round pastry cutter, cut circles from each bread slice. (Reserve scraps for crumbs.) In a small saucepan melt butter and add thyme. Brush bread circles with this mixture. Place on a cookie sheet and bake 10 minutes, until golden. Combine shrimp with cheese, bread crumbs, mayonnaise and salt. When circles are cool, put a rounded tablespoon of shrimp mixture on each. Sprinkle with a pinch of dill and place under broiler for about 3 minutes.

SERVES: 20

Mardi Gras Cooking

Mom's Shrimp

Submitted by Orlene S. James (via Shelly James)
Mt. Solon, Virginia

INGREDIENTS:

½ cup butter, melted
1 medium onion, chopped fine
Juice of ½ lemon
1 tablespoon Worcestershire sauce
2 dashes Tabasco sauce

5 bay leaves
½ package pickling spice
1 pound large shrimp, peeled and de-
    veined
Water to cover shrimp

Put melted butter in a small saucepan and add onion. Simmer until onion is soft. Add lemon juice, Worcestershire, and Tabasco, and mix. Leave warm and set aside the sauce.

In large pot, boil water with bay leaves and pickling spice. Turn down to simmer and add shrimp. Cook until shrimp are pink (about 5-7 minutes). Drain off water, spice and bay leaves. Serve with bowl of warm sauce in middle of shrimp.

SERVES: 8

Family recipe

Spinach Cheese Squares

Submitted by Maria Romhilt
Richmond, Virginia

INGREDIENTS:

3 eggs
1 cup milk
1 cup flour
1 teaspoon baking powder
1 teaspoon seasoned salt
1 tablespoon chopped onion

2 10-ounce packages chopped spinach —
   thawed and drained
½ pound Monterey Jack cheese —grated
¼ pound Monterey Jack cheese with
   jalapeños, grated
2 tablespoons butter

Beat eggs with fork in large bowl. Add milk, flour, baking powder, salt and onion and mix well. Add spinach and all cheese and mix.

Place butter in 9″ × 13″ baking dish and heat to melt. Spread in bottom of dish. Add spinach mixture. Bake at 350° F for 35–40 minutes. Allow to cool and cut into squares. Squares freeze well, and can be heated in microwave.

Note: For a stronger jalapeño flavor, use ¾ pound Monterey Jack cheese with jalapeño instead of ½ pound plain Monterey Jack, plus ¼ pound of Monterey Jack with jalapeños.

SERVES: About 90 1″ squares.

Adapted from *Stuffed Cougar Cookbook*

Tuna Cheese Ball

Submitted by Carol Jarett
Richmond, Virginia

INGREDIENTS:

1 6-ounce can chunk light tuna
2 tablespoons minced onion
1 8-ounce package cream cheese,
   softened

1½ teaspoons garlic powder
½ cup chopped fresh parsley

Drain tuna, and flake in bowl. Add softened cream cheese, onion and garlic powder, and mix together thoroughly. Turn out onto waxed paper, and shape into ball. Refrigerate overnight. Before serving, roll in chopped parsley. Serve with assorted crackers.

SERVES: About 8

Friend's recipe

Cooked Spinach Balls

Submitted by Deane R. Dubansky
Richmond, Virginia

INGREDIENTS:

2 10-ounce packages of frozen
   chopped spinach
2 cups herb bread stuffing
1 large onion, grated
4 eggs, beaten

½ cup grated Parmesan cheese
¾ cup melted margarine
1½ teaspoons dried thyme
½ teaspoon garlic salt
¼ teaspoon pepper

Cook spinach according to package direction. Squeeze out *all* liquid. Mix, by hand, drained spinach with stuffing mix, onion, eggs, cheese, margarine, thyme, garlic salt and pepper. Chill at least two hours. (Can be chilled overnight and rolled the next day). Roll into 1-inch balls. Bake in 350° F preheated oven (spray the cookie sheet with non-stick spray) until outside is crispy and bubbly, about 10 minutes. Serve with sweet hot mustard.

If desired, Spinach Balls may be shaped, frozen on cookie sheets until hard (uncooked) and then transferred into freezer bags. Let them defrost before cooking.

YIELDS: approximately 60

Family recipe

Veggie Quesadillas

Submitted by Kathy Burns

INGREDIENTS:

1 cup salsa (roasted bell pepper is good)
1 cup drained canned black beans
1 zucchini, shredded

8 (6 inch) flour tortillas
¾ cup shredded Monterey Jack cheese
   (use jalapeno-style for extra flavor)

In medium bowl, combine salsa, beans and zucchini. Spread ¼ of the mixture over each of 4 tortillas. Top each portion with 3 tablespoons cheese, cover each with another tortilla.

Heat an 8–10 inch nonstick skillet over medium heat. One at a time, carefully cook each quesadilla, turning once, until cheese is melted and tortilla is slightly browned. Cut each quesadilla into quarters and serve immediately.

YIELDS: 16 quarters

Friend's recipe

Tasty Treats

Submitted by Alice Clark
Midlothian, Virginia

INGREDIENTS:

1 bag (8–10 ounces) stick pretzels
1 box cheese tid bits
4 tablespoons Worcestershire sauce
4 tablespoons Accent
1 pound mixed salted nuts
Garlic powder

1 small box Wheat Chex
1 small box Cheerios
1 stick melted butter
4 tablespoons seasoning salt
1 small can cashews

Into large roasting pan put butter and Worcestershire sauce, pretzels, tid bits, Wheat Chex and Cheerios. Stir well. Bake at 225° for 2½ hours. Remove from oven — sprinkle with Accent and seasoning salt. Add mixed nuts and cashews and garlic powder to taste. Mix. Bake extra ½ hour.

YIELD: Lots!

Family recipe

Roquefort Toasts

Submitted by Jane Whitaker
Richmond, Virginia

INGREDIENTS:

1 round loaf country style bread or
    French baguette or Italian loaf, cut
    into ½ inch thick slices

MIX:

4 ounces Roquefort, crumbled and
    softened
2 tablespoons unsalted butter, softened

1 teaspoon minced garlic
½ teaspoon Worcestershire
Freshly ground pepper

Preheat oven to 375° F. Arrange bread slices in one layer on a cookie sheet and toast in middle of oven for 4 minutes. Spread each toast with a thin layer of cheese mixture and bake in oven an additional 5 minutes or until cheese is melted.

As hors d'oeuvres, top with sliced apple or pear. Also good with soup or salad or cut up as croutons.

SERVES: Depends on size of bread slices.

Family Recipe

Crazy Mixed-Up Popcorn

Submitted by Jennie Fritz
Virginia Beach, Virginia

INGREDIENTS:

6 cups popped popcorn
3 cups crisp rice cereal squares
2 cups toasted oat O-shaped cereal
1½ cups dry roasted peanuts
1 cup pecan pieces

1 cup firmly packed brown sugar
½ cup butter or margarine
¼ cup light corn syrup
1 teaspoon vanilla extract
¼ teaspoon baking soda

Stir together popcorn, rice cereal, toasted oat cereal, peanuts and pecans in a lightly greased roasting pan.

Bring brown sugar, butter, and corn syrup to a boil in a 3-quart saucepan over medium heat, stirring constantly: boil, without stirring, 5 minutes or until a candy thermometer registers 250 degrees. Remove from heat: stir in vanilla and soda. Pour over popcorn mixture, and stir until coated.

Bake at 250° F for 1 hour, stirring every 20 minutes. Cool in pan on a wire rack: Break apart. Store in an airtight container.

YIELDS: 14 cups

Friend's recipe

Cheese Chips

Submitted by Alice Clark
Midlothian, Virginia

INGREDIENTS:

½ pound butter
½ pound N.Y. State cheese, grated
2 cups flour
½ teaspoon salt

Dash red pepper
1 egg white, beaten stiff
1 cup pecan pieces

Soften butter, add cheese, blend in flour and salt. Roll into balls. Flatten with fork. Put whipped egg white on top. Sprinkle with salt. Top with pecan pieces. Bake 350° F for 10 to 12 minutes.

YIELDS: about 66 chips

Source unknown

Bruschetta

Submitted by Abby Swanson
Richmond, Virginia

INGREDIENTS:

1 red onion
8 roma tomatoes
4 tablespoons minced garlic

4 tablespoons olive oil
Crumbled feta cheese (optional)
1 loaf French baguette bread

Chop red onion and tomatoes into small squares. Combine onion, garlic, and olive oil in a large saucepan. Sauté over medium heat until onions turn clear. Slice and toast baguette bread. When onions are clear, add chopped tomatoes and continue to sauté on medium for 3 minutes. Use a spoon to place bruschetta onto toasted bread and sprinkle feta over top. Enjoy.

SERVES: 10 to 12

Family recipe

Cranberry Meat Balls

Submitted by Louise Creeger
Richmond, Virginia

INGREDIENTS:

2 pounds ground beef
3 eggs
1 medium onion, diced
½ cup matzo meal
1½ teaspoons salt
¼ teaspoon pepper

1 can (6 ounces) tomato paste
1½ cups water
1 16-ounce can whole berry cranberry
  sauce
2 tablespoons catsup

Mix meat, eggs, onion, matzo meal, salt and pepper and form into small balls.

Combine paste, water, cranberry sauce, catsup in Dutch oven. Mix well and bring to full boil, stirring frequently. Add the meat balls and simmer covered on low heat for 2 hours.

Note: Can be served as main course make large meatballs and serve over noodles.

SERVES: 8 to 10 for appetizer

Family recipe

Crescent Vegetable Pizzas

Submitted by Jennie Fritz
Richmond, Virginia

INGREDIENTS:

2 large packages crescent rolls
2 8-ounce packages cream cheese
1 cup mayonnaise
1 package original ranch dressing

Small pieces of: broccoli, cauliflower, green onion, tomatoes, cucumber, carrots or any vegetables of your choice

Place crescent rolls on cookie sheet, flatten and seal perforated edges together. Bake 10–15 minutes (lowest time on package) at temperature specified on package. Cool.

Mix: 2 8-ounce cream cheese, 1 cup mayonnaise, 1 package original ranch dressing.

Spread this mixture on top of cooled crescent rolls.

Cut into small pieces: broccoli, cauliflower, green onions, tomatoes, cucumber, carrots (or any vegetable you desire).

Sprinkle vegetables on top of cream cheese. Press down. Refrigerate. Cut into small squares.

SERVES: approximately 20

Friend's recipe

Roasted Red Pepper Biscuits

Submitted by Katie Hudson
Ruther Glen, Virginia

INGREDIENTS:

1 package jumbo refrigerator biscuits
2 ounces roasted red peppers in oil
¼ cup hard salami

¼ cup Parmesan cheese, grated
¼ cup butter or margarine, melted
Cooking spray

Spray a 9-inch square baking pan with cooking spray. Cut biscuits into 6 pieces each and place in baking pan (OK for biscuits to touch). Place roasted pepper and salami in a food processor; pulse until the meat is finely chopped. Spread the pepper and salami mix evenly over the biscuits. Sprinkle with Parmesan cheese. Drizzle butter over the top of the biscuits. Bake at 350° F until lightly browned and bubbling (about 12 minutes). Serve immediately.

SERVES: 18

Original recipe

Stuffe∂ Mushrooms

Submitted by Sallie Grant
Richmond, Virginia

INGREDIENTS:

1 package thawed Stouffer's spinach souffle
1 cup untoasted bread crumbs
2 teaspoons lemon juice
1 teaspoon minced onion

½ teaspoon salt
24 large mushroom caps
Melted butter
Parmesan cheese

Preheat oven to 375° F. Rinse mushrooms and remove stems. Mix thawed spinach souffle, bread crumbs, lemon juice, onion and salt together. Stuff the 24 large mushroom caps with spinach mixture. Brush with melted butter and sprinkle with Parmesan cheese.

Bake in 375° F oven for 15–18 minutes.

SERVES: 8 to 12

Family recipe

Cantaloupe with Lime an∂ Mint

Submitted by "Sunny" Adams
Richmond, Virginia

INGREDIENTS:

1 cantaloupe
½ cup sugar
½ cup water

2 tablespoons fresh lime juice
¼ cup coarsely chopped fresh mint

In a small non-reactive saucepan, bring sugar and water to a boil over moderately high heat. Lower heat and simmer until sugar is dissolved, about 3 minutes. Let cool completely. Stir in lime juice and mint. Cover and refrigerate until chilled, at least 1 hour.

Peel cantaloupe and cut into cubes. Place in bowl and pour chilled lime-mint syrup over. Toss gently to combine and serve.

SERVES: 8 to 10

Ol∂ Britton Hills Farm Cookbook

Caramelized Onion, Apple and Brie Tartlets

Submitted by Babs Jackson,
President/CEO, HHH

INGREDIENTS:

2 tablespoons olive oil

7 cups thinly sliced white onions (about 3 medium)

1½ tablespoons minced fresh thyme

1 sheet frozen puff pastry (half of 17.3 ounce package)

1 6-ounce Granny Smith apple, peeled, quartered, cored, thinly sliced crosswise

2 6-ounce wedges chilled Brie cheese, rind removed, cheese cut into ¼-inch-thick slices, each slice cut crosswise into thirds

Heat oil in heavy large skillet over medium heat. Add onions and sauté until deep golden brown, about 30 minutes. Mix in thyme. Season with salt and pepper to taste. Cool. Can be prepared 1 day ahead. Cover and refrigerate.

Roll out pastry on lightly floured work surface to 12-inch square. Cut pastry lengthwise into six 2-inch-wide strips. Cut strips crosswise into six 2-inch squares, for a total of 36 squares. Place pastry squares, spacing apart, on 2 large baking sheets. (Can be prepared 1 day ahead. Cover and refrigerate.)

Preheat oven to 350° F. Spoon 1½ teaspoons onion mixture atop each pastry square. Top with 2 apple slices. Bake until pastry is golden brown, about 20 minutes. Top each square with 1 piece cheese and bake just until cheese melts, about 3 minutes. Transfer to platter.

For appetizers size portions, roll pastry to approximately 9-inch square, cut into 9 3-inch squares. Divide onion among 9 pastries, top with 3 apples slices (sliced lengthwise) and bake for 20 minutes as above. Place 2 strips of Brie over apples and bake just until cheese melts, about 3 minutes. Transfer to individual plates.

YIELDS: 36 hors d'oeuvres or 9 appetizer portions.

Adapted from *Bon Appetit*

Holiday Mocha Punch

Submitted by Eddy Gelrud
Richmond, Virginia

INGREDIENTS:

¼ cup coffee powder (instant)
⅔ cup Hershey syrup
2 quarts milk

3 pints vanilla ice cream
1½ cups whipped cream
2 cups rum or bourbon

Stir coffee powder and chocolate syrup into milk and chill. Soften ice cream and place in a punch bowl. Stir in coffee mixture, whipped cream and rum or bourbon. Serve immediately.

SERVES: 10

Friend's recipe—Jane Dunck

Sangría

Submitted by Jeannine Daniel
Midlothian, Virginia

INGREDIENTS:

1 can frozen whisky sour mix—if not
    available, freeze approximately
    12 ounces liquid whiskey sour mix
½ cup Jim Beam bourbon
1 fifth rosé wine

1 quart cranberry cocktail
1 quart sparkling water
Garnish with slices of orange, lemon, lime,
    seedless grapes, strawberries

Mix all ingredients.

Note: If doubling recipe, use 1 quart sparkling water and 1 quart Fresca

SERVES: 18 — 6-ounce size glasses

Former teacher

Poppa's Bourbon Recipe

Submitted by Nancy G. Powell
Richmond, Virginia

INGREDIENTS:

2 small tea bags
2 cups water
2 cups sugar
1-6 ounce frozen orange juice

1-6 ounce frozen lemonaide
1½ cups bourbon
6½ cups water

Bring 2 cups water to a boil; add tea bags, remove from heat, cover and let sit for 15 minutes.

Remove tea bags; add sugar, orange juice, lemonade, bourbon, and 6½ cups water. Mix well, pour into suitable freezer container(s) and freeze until slushy. Serve in old fashion glasses with orange and lemon garnish.

SERVES: 12±

Family recipe

Hot Wassail Drink

Submitted by Barbara Sanford
Chesterfield, Virginia

INGREDIENTS:

4 cinnamon sticks
1 tablespoon allspice
2 cups water
1 gallon apple cider
1 quart pineapple juice

1 quart orange juice
½ pint bottled lemon juice
1 quart strong tea
1 cup brown sugar
½ cup honey

Simmer 4 sticks cinnamon, 1 tablespoon allspice and 2 cups water until taste is out of cinnamon sticks, approximately 15 to 20 minutes.

In 2 gallon container, combine apple cider, pineapple juice, orange juice, lemon juice, tea, brown sugar and honey. Strain cinnamon mixture into cider/juice mixture. Stir. Will keep indefinitely in refrigerator. Heat before serving.

SERVES: Approximately 32 1-cup servings.

Family recipe

Coffee Punch

Submitted by Babs Jackson,
President/CEO, HHH

INGREDIENTS:

6 tablespoons instant coffee
1 cup boiling water
1 cup sugar

3 cups milk
2 quarts gingerale
1 quart vanilla ice cream

Dissolve coffee in hot water, add sugar and milk, stirring until dissolved, put in ice cream and pour in gingerale.

SERVES: 35

Source unknown

Soups
and
Sandwiches

Black Bean and Pineapple Quesadillas

Submitted by Louis Mahoney
Richmond, Virginia

INGREDIENTS:

1 can (15 ounce) black beans, rinsed and drained

1 can (8 ounce) crushed pineapple, drained

8 tablespoons prepared salsa

Chopped fresh cilantro, to taste

8 (8-inch) flour tortillas

1 cup (4 ounces) shredded Cheddar cheese

Sour cream

Combine beans, pineapple, 6 teaspoons salsa and cilantro (if desired). Spread ½ cup bean mixture over 4 tortillas. Top each with ¼ of the cheese. Top with another tortilla. Cook over medium-high heat, in non-stick skillet, for a minute or two on each side, or until cheese melts. Cut each quesadilla into six wedges. Place three wedges on each plate, top with remaining salsa and a dollop of sour cream.

SERVES: 8

Adapted from Dole Food Co.

Cold Cream of Cucumber Soup

Submitted by Ann Bendheim
Richmond, Virginia

INGREDIENTS:

2 large or 3 medium cucumbers
1 medium onion, chopped
1 cup chicken broth
2 tablespoons flour
¼ teaspoon white pepper

½ teaspoon salt
Dash of garlic powder
1 cup sour cream
Dill weed

Pare, seed, and coarsely chop cucumbers. Place all ingredients except sour cream and dill weed in blender, blend until smooth. Add sour cream; chill. Sprinkle dill weed on top before serving or float a slice of cucumber.

SERVES: 4 to 6

Soupcon Cookbook

Cold Summer Squash Soup

Submitted by Maryglyn McGraw
Richmond, Virginia

INGREDIENTS:

1 pound summer squash
1 medium onion (optional)
3 cups chicken broth

3-ounce size cream cheese
Curry powder
Sour cream for garnish

Slice onion and squash. Cook in chicken broth until soft. Cool slightly. Add cream cheese. Pureé in blender or Cuisanart. Add curry powder to taste. Chill. Serve with dollop of sour cream.

YIELDS: approximately 6 to 8 cups

Friend Candy Materne Jones's recipe

Velvet Pea and Zucchini Soup

Submitted by Mary Guthrie
Richmond, Virginia

INGREDIENTS:

¾ pound zucchini, chopped
⅓ cup finely chopped onion
⅓ cup finely chopped scallion, white
    part only
2 tablespoons vegetable oil

⅛ teaspoon dried thyme
1½ cups chicken broth (canned)
1 10-ounce package frozen peas, thawed
Sour cream for garnish

In heavy large saucepan, cook zucchini, onion, and scallion in oil over moderate heat, stirring for 3 minutes. Add thyme, broth, and 1 cup water. Bring to boil and simmer, covered for 6 minutes.

Add peas and simmer, uncovered, for 6 minutes, or until vegetables are tender. Transfer about ⅓ cup of peas to a small bowl, reserving for garnish. In a blender, pureé the mixture in batches, and season with salt and pepper. Serve warm or at room temperature. Garnish with dollop of sour cream and some of reserved peas.

SERVES: 4

Gourmet Magazine

Easy Gazpacho

Submitted by Victoria R. Beam
Chester, Virginia

INGREDIENTS:

1 46-ounce can V8 juice
1 large peeled, thickly sliced cucumber
1 large sweet white onion
½ cup best quality olive oil

4–5 tablespoons good vinegar
Salt and fresh-ground pepper to taste
2–3 cloves garlic, to taste
1 medium sweet green Bell pepper

Blend all ingredients except green pepper. Best to stop while cucumber and onion bits are small but still visible. (Consistency will be creamy.)

Add diced green pepper for crunchiness and dashes of Tabasco sauce to taste.

Chill. Flavor develops best by second day. Keep refrigerated. Will last.

SERVES: 8

Friend's recipe

Seafood Chowder

Submitted by Ann Bendheim
Richmond, Virginia

INGREDIENTS:

Bacon, 12 slices
Onions, 1 cup chopped
Celery, 1 cup chopped
½ lemon
1 clove garlic, thinly sliced
1 quart water
2 #2 cans tomatoes
¼ cup catsup
¼ teaspoon curry powder

2 teaspoons salt
⅛ teaspoon Tabasco
1 tablespoon Worcestershire sauce
1 pound scallops
1 pound fish—halibut, haddock or cod
1 pound shrimp
⅔ cup sherry
4 tablespoons margarine

In a 4 quart kettle, snip bacon in small pieces. Cook over low heat until brown, stirring occasionally. Add chopped onions and celery. Cover, cook 5 minutes.

Cut lemon into thin slices, quarter and remove seeds; add lemon, garlic, water, tomatoes, catsup, curry powder, salt, Tabasco, and Worcestershire sauce to kettle. Bring to boil, then reduce heat and cook slowly for about 30 minutes.

If scallops are large, cut into smaller pieces; peel shell from uncooked shrimp; rinse in cold water, drain them well. Add scallops and shrimp to chowder and cook over low heat for about 20 minutes.

Cut fish into one-inch pieces. Add to chowder along with sherry and butter. Cook 10 minutes or until fish is tender.

SERVES: 8 to 10

Friend Frances Alspaugh's recipe

Creamy Onion Soup

Submitted by Annette Gelber
Richmond, Virginia

INGREDIENTS:

1 pound fresh mushrooms, washed
    and dried
⅓ ounce dried Italian mushrooms
½ cup lukewarm water
3 tablespoons olive oil
¼ cup butter
2 garlic cloves, mashed

¼ cup diced onion
Pinch of black pepper
Pinch of cayenne pepper
5 cups boiling beef broth
½ cup dry sherry
Salt
½ cup heavy cream

Clean mushrooms. Remove stems; chop fine. Slice caps thin; chop coarsely. Soak the dried mushrooms in the lukewarm water. Drain; save the water; chop mushrooms.

Place olive oil in medium-size saucepan; heat; add garlic. Stir well to extract flavor of garlic. Discard bits of garlic; add onion and sauté until medium brown. Add the dried mushrooms with water, chopped stems and fresh mushrooms; sauté slowly in butter for 15 minutes. Add black and cayenne pepper, beef broth and sherry. Add salt to taste if needed. Bring to a rapid boil for 5 minutes. Remove from heat and stir in cream. Serve immediately.

SERVES: 4 to 5

Leone's Italian Cookbook

Plantation Peanut Soup

Submitted by Nancy G. Powell
Richmond, Virginia

INGREDIENTS:

3 cups chicken broth (low sodium)
1 cup peanut butter*
⅛ teaspoon celery salt
⅛ teaspoon garlic salt

½ teaspoon sugar
1⅓ cup cream
Chopped peanuts, garnish

Heat broth to boiling. Add peanut butter, stirring until smooth. Add salts and sugar; stir in cream. Heat, but DO NOT BOIL. Top each serving with chopped peanuts.

*If you prefer a thicker base, increase peanut butter by ¼ cup.

SERVES: 4 to 6

Friend Katie Surdyk's recipe

Chicken Lemon Soup

Submitted by Nancy G. Powell
Richmond, Virginia

INGREDIENTS:

4 cups chicken broth
4 tablespoons fresh lemon juice
Seeded whole lemon, thinly sliced,
    to garnish

4 eggs
½ cup thick cream

Heat broth to boiling. Beat eggs with whisk until light. Beat in lemon juice. Slowly pour 2 cups of hot broth into egg/lemon mixture, stirring constantly. Pour egg mixture into remaining broth in saucepan, stirring with whisk as soup thickens over low heat—about 4 minutes. Garnish each serving with thin lemon slice.

SERVES: 4

Friend Katie Surdyk's recipe

Black Bean and Corn Chowder

Submitted by Stephanie Schonauer
Huntington Beach, California

INGREDIENTS:

15 ounces black beans, rinsed and drained
14 ounces can diced tomatoes or whole
    tomatoes chopped
10 ounce box frozen corn kernels
Small onion, finely chopped

2 cups milk
4 cups water
¼ teaspoon garlic powder
Salt and pepper to taste

Heat all ingredients together in a large pot over medium heat for 25 minutes. Serve warm.

SERVES: 4 to 6

Source unknown

Sweet Red Pepper Soup with Crab

Submitted by Carol Holt
Richmond, Virginia

INGREDIENTS:

6 red peppers
Sea salt

1 quart heavy cream
12 ounces crabmeat

Split, seed and cut peppers into quarters. Put in pan and add cream. Simmer 15 minutes. Blend in blender until creamy. Put through screen colander and squeeze out as much liquid as possible. Add salt. This is what makes it sweet. Serve in bowls sprinkled with crab.

SERVES: 6

Friend's recipe

Old English Cheese Soup

Submitted by Babs Jackson,
President/CEO, HHH

INGREDIENTS:

4 cups grated carrots
4 cups grated onion
4 cups chopped celery
½ cup butter

2 cups flour
8 cups milk
8 cups chicken broth
64 ounces Old English cheese

Saute carrots, onions and celery in butter. Blend milk, flour and chicken broth in double boiler. Add vegetables. Heat. Add sliced Old English cheese and stir till cheese melts.

Note: One-fourth recipe about the right amount for 6–8 servings.

SERVES: 30

Source unknown

Vegetable Beef Soup

Submitted by Debi Somerville
Fredericksburg, Virginia

INGREDIENTS:

1 pound lean ground beef
1 cup chopped onion
1 cup chopped celery
1 can (28 ounces) whole tomatoes
    undrained, chopped
1 can (28 ounces) water

1½ cups water
3 beef bouillon cubes
1 teaspoon salt
½ teaspoon basil
¼ teaspoon black pepper
1 pound frozen soup vegetables

In 3-quart saucepan cook beef until no longer pink, drain off any excess fat. Add all ingredients except frozen vegetables. Bring to a boil, reduce heat and simmer 2 hours. Add frozen vegetables and cook only until frozen vegetables are tender.

You can use this soup for a base and add any vegetables (fresh or frozen), beans (canned and drained) or pasta/noodles/rice.

Note: Soup can be frozen.

SERVES: 8 to 10

Original recipe

Alive and Raw Tomato Soup

Submitted by Lynda Carter
Petersburg, Virginia

INGREDIENTS:

8 sundried tomatoes
4 ripe tomatoes
½ cup olive oil
2 cloves garlic

1 sprig basil
12 ounces of water
1 date
1 pinch cayenne pepper

Soak sundried tomatoes in water at room temperature for 2 hours. Place soaked tomatoes in blender with ripe tomatoes, garlic, basil, date, pepper and water. Blend till smooth. Add olive oil, blend for 2 minutes. Soup will thicken. Serve at room temperature.

SERVES: 2 to 4

Original recipe

Paul's Spinach Soup

Submitted by Pat Glupker
Richmond, Virginia

INGREDIENTS:

1 3-ounce package chicken Ramen noodles
1 10-ounce package frozen chopped
    spinach

4 cups water
Parmesan cheese

Gently crush package of noodles to break apart. Remove seasoning packet and add with spinach to water in pan. Cover and heat until spinach is tender. A few minutes before serving, add noodles. Cover and heat briefly until noodles soften. Serve in soup bowls topped with Parmesan cheese.

SERVES: 4

Original recipe

Easy Vegetable Chowder

Submitted by Annette Gelber
Richmond, Virginia

INGREDIENTS:

11 new potatoes
2 large carrots
1 large onion
3 tablespoons olive oil
2 (10¾ ounce) cans condensed Cheddar
    cheese soup, undiluted
4 cups water

1 (1.15 ounce) envelope dry onion
    soup mix
1 teaspoon pepper
½ cup sliced green onion
Garnishes: whole or sliced green onions,
    shredded Cheddar cheese

Cut potatoes into ½ inch cubes and carrots into ½ inch slices; coarsely chop onions. Saute vegetables in hot oil in a Dutch oven until tender.

Stir together Cheddar cheese soup, 4 cups water, dry onion soup mix and 1 teaspoon pepper until blended, add to vegetable mixture. Bring to a boil; reduce heat and simmer 30 minutes. Stir in ½ cup sliced green onions just before serving. Garnish.

YIELDS: 6 cups

Adapted from *Southern Living*

Minestrone Soup

Submitted by Bev Dillard
Richmond, Virginia

INGREDIENTS:

1 cup chopped onion
1½ pounds Italian sausage-slit casings or
slice (turkey ok)
6 cups broth-beef bouillon
½ cup red wine
1 pound can tomato juice
1 cup ketchup or 1 large can crushed
tomatoes
2 cups sliced carrots

1 cup sliced celery
1 teaspoon Italian seasoning or oregano
2 cloves garlic crushed or more to taste
2 medium zucchini sliced
1 medium red or green pepper chopped
¼ cup parsley chopped, fresh flat leaf best
½ package frozen tortellini or 2 packages
fresh (bagged or boxed ok)

Brown onions, then combine all ingredients but tortellini. Simmer uncovered, then add pasta to cook according to package directions. Optional: top with grated Parmesan cheese.

SERVES: 10

Source unknown

Clam Chowder

Submitted by Elizabeth Jordan
Gloucester Point, Virginia

INGREDIENTS:

30 fresh clams, minced
2 strips bacon, cut into small pieces
2 small potatoes, cubed
1 cup tomatoes, diced

1 teaspoon seafood seasoning
1 onion, chopped
1 cup water or clam juice

Boil bacon, potatoes, tomatoes, seasoning, onion and water or clam juice (all, except clams) about 45 minutes. Add clams and boil an additional 15 minutes.

SERVES: 2

Family recipe

Scotch Broth

Submitted by Annette Gelber
Richmond, Virginia

INGREDIENTS:

2 to 3 pounds neck of lamb
½ cup pearl barley
2 quarts water
1 teaspoon salt
¼ teaspoon pepper

2 carrots
1 turnip
2 stalks celery, finely diced
12 tiny onions, peeled
6 teaspoons chopped parsley

Put lamb and barley in large pot and add water. Cover and simmer 2½ hours. Strain and chill broth to bring fat to top. Remove fat and discard. Pick out bones and discard. Cut meat into small pieces and return meat and barley to broth. Add 1 teaspoon salt and ¼ teaspoon pepper. Peel and dice carrots and turnip and add with celery and onions to broth. Cook 1 hour longer, or until vegetables are thoroughly done and soup is well blended. Season to taste.

SERVES: 6

Adapted from *Woman's Day* Magazine (1965)

Ham and 4 C's Soup

Submitted by Debi Somerville
Fredericksburg, Virginia

INGREDIENTS:

1 ham bone
½ pound frozen corn kernels
½ head cabbage
3 carrots, sliced

3 celery stalks, sliced
1 large onion, chopped
Salt and pepper to taste
Hot sauce, to taste

Cover leftover ham bone with water, bring to a boil and simmer until meat comes off freely. (1 to 2 hours.) Remove ham bone, strain liquid in pan and return this liquid to the pan. Add all vegetables except corn, bring back to a boil, reduce heat and simmer until vegetables are tender. Taste when vegetables become tender and season with salt and pepper and hot sauce (a few drops at a time) add corn and cook only until corn is tender. Scrape ham from bone and return ham to pot.

SERVES: 4 to 8

Friend Cathy Hanbury's recipe

Hot Shrimp Sandwich

Submitted by Nancy Pendergast
Richmond, Virginia

INGREDIENTS:

Juice ½ lemon
¼ cup chopped onion
4 hard boiled eggs, diced
Thousand Island dressing

6 slices bread
1 pound small shrimp, cooked
Parmesan cheese
1 cup mozzarella cheese, shredded

Mix together lemon juice, onions, and diced eggs. Spread dressing on slices of bread, then spread the egg mixture on top of bread slices.

Next place the cooked shrimp evenly on top of egg mixture. Sprinkle a little Parmesan cheese over this and finally top all with mozzarella cheese. (May prepare to this point and then heat near serving time.)

Broil on cookie sheet till golden and bubbly.

SERVES: 6

Adapted from *Harmony Grove Cookbook*

Turkey-Pastrami and Cheese Stack

Submitted by Annette Gelber
Richmond, Virginia

INGREDIENTS:

8 slices pumpernickel bread
¼ cup hot horseradish mustard
1 pound thinly sliced turkey pastrami

½ pound thinly sliced Swiss cheese
1 cup broccoli sprouts, packed

Spread each slice of pumpernickel with ½ tablespoon horseradish mustard. Divide the turkey pastrami and Swiss cheese into eight equal portions. Arrange one portion of the pastrami on four of the slices, then top each with one portion of the Swiss cheese. Repeat layering with the remaining pastrami and cheese. Divide broccoli sprouts even among the sandwiches. Top with remaining slices of bread. Cut the sandwiches in half and serve.

SERVES: 4

Adapted from *First* Magazine

Roasted Vegetable and Cheese Panini

Submitted by Cathy B. Hinton
Midlothian, Virginia

INGREDIENTS:

ROASTED VEGETABLES:

1 small zucchini, cut in thin lengthwise
    pieces
1 Portabello mushroom cap, sliced
¼ red onion, cut in wedges
½ yellow pepper, cut in strips

½ cup grape tomatoes
1 to 2 tablespoons lowfat or nonfat
    Italian dressing
Kosher salt

4 slices French bread, sliced diagonally
Dijon mustard

2 slices Havarti Dill cheese (or your
    favorite cheese)
Olive oil

In a large bowl combine zucchini, mushroom, onion, pepper and tomatoes. Add Italian dressing; stir to coat vegetables. Spread vegetables in single layer on baking pan; sprinkle with salt. Roast in 425° F oven 30 minutes, stirring once or twice, or until vegetables start to brown. Spread mustard on top sides of bread; layer roasted vegetables and cheese on 2 slices of bread. Top with remaining bread. Brush outer sides of bread with oil. Place sandwiches in heated grill. Close top and grill until golden brown and cheese has melted.

YIELDS: 2 sandwiches

Original recipe

Italian Heroines

Submitted by Annette Gelber
Richmond, Virginia

INGREDIENTS:

1 teaspoon olive oil
8 ounces mushrooms, sliced ¼" thick
1 cup thinly sliced onions
4 hero (hoagie or sub) rolls, split
6 tablespoons reduced-fat basil pesto sauce

8 ounces sliced, cooked turkey
2 cups deli-style marinated, roasted red
   peppers
1 cup (4 ounces) shredded mozzarella
   cheese

Heat oven to 425° F. Have a cookie sheet ready.

Heat oil in a large non-stick skillet over medium-high heat. Add mushrooms and onion; saute 5 to 7 minutes, stirring often, until lightly browned.

Meanwhile spread cut sides of rolls with pesto. Top with turkey and peppers. Spoon on onion and mushrooms and sprinkle with cheese. Bake 5 minutes or until cheese melts.

SERVES: 4

Adapted from *Woman's Day* (1999)

Ham and Spinach Focaccia Sandwiches

Submitted by Annette Gelber
Richmond, Virginia

INGREDIENTS:

3 tablespoons low fat mayonnaise
2 tablespoons fresh chopped basil
2 teaspoons sun dried tomato sprinkles
¼ teaspoon crushed red pepper
1 (8 inch) round focaccia bread (about
   8 ounces)

8 ounces smoked deli ham, thinly sliced
1 bottle (7 ounces) roasted red bell
   peppers, drained and sliced
1 cup spinach leaves

Combine the mayonnaise, basil, sun dried tomato sprinkles and red pepper in small bowl. Cut bread in half horizontally. Spread mayonnaise mixture over the cut sides of bread. Place ham over bottom half of bread. Top with peppers and spinach and cover with top half of bread. Cut the focaccia crosswise into 4 wedges.

SERVES: 4

Cooking Light Magazine

Oven-Grilled Reuben Sandwiches

Submitted by Annette Gelber
Richmond, Virginia

INGREDIENTS:

2 cups sauerkraut, drained
¾ teaspoon caraway seeds
1¾ cups Thousand Island Dressing
12 rye bread slices without seeds

6 pumpernickel bread slices
12 (1 ounce) Swiss cheese slices
48 thin slices corned beef (1½ pounds)

Stir together sauerkraut and caraway seeds.

Spread dressing evenly on 1 side of each bread slice. Layer 6 rye bread slices and 6 pumpernickel slices evenly with cheese, sauerkraut mixture and corned beef. Stack to make 6 (2 layer) sandwiches, ending with remaining rye bread slices.

Coat a baking sheet with vegetable cooking spray. Arrange sandwiches on baking sheet. Coat bottom of a second sheet with cooking spray and place coated side down on top of corned beef sandwiches.

Bake sandwiches at 475° F for 15 to 20 minutes or until golden and cheese is slightly melted. Serve warm.

SERVES: 6

Adapted from *Southern Living* Magazine

Grilled Cheese and Chicken Sandwiches

Submitted by Patty Giles
Richmond, Virginia

INGREDIENTS:

2 cups chopped cooked chicken
⅓ cup golden raisins
¼ cup slivered almonds, toasted
¼ cup diced celery

½ cup mayonnaise
12 slices Monterey Jack cheese
12 whole wheat bread slices
¼ cup butter or margarine

Stir together chicken, raisins, almonds, celery and mayonnaise. Place 1 cheese slice on each of 6 bread slices, spread chicken mixture evenly over each and top with remaining cheese and bread slices. Spread half of butter evenly on 1 side of each sandwich. Cook buttered side down in a nonstick skillet until lightly browned. Turn sandwich and spread with remaining butter and cook until lightly browned. Serve immediately.

YIELDS: 6 sandwiches

Source unknown

Middle Eastern Lamb Pocket

Submitted by Annette Gelber
Richmond, Virginia

INGREDIENTS:

1 pound lamb top round, cut into 1" cubes
1 cucumber, halved
1 container (4 ounces) cucumber-dill
    cheese spread

2 tomatoes, sliced
4 pita pockets, halved
Salt and pepper to taste

Season lamb with salt and pepper. In large skillet, over medium-high heat, brown lamb cubes, turning occasionally for 10 minutes or until cooked through. Meanwhile, remove seeds from one half of the cucumber and dice. Slice other half.

In bowl, combine diced cucumber and cheese spread, season with salt and pepper. Evenly divide lamb, cucumber spread, cucumbers and tomatoes among pita pockets. If desired, serve with sliced red onion and chopped mint.

SERVES: 4

Adapted from *First* Magazine

Salads, Dressings, and Condiments

Pineapple-Shrimp Salad with Roquefort Cheese

Submitted by Babs Jackson,
President/CEO, HHH

INGREDIENTS:

1 large fresh pineapple
¾ pound cooked, shelled shrimp
   (medium size)
Romaine lettuce
⅓ cup crumbled Roquefort cheese

1 cup sour cream
¼ cup mayonnaise
3 tablespoons cream
Salt
Paprika

Cube pineapple into bite-size pieces; toss with shrimp. Arrange romaine on individual plates; top with pineapple mixture.

Mash cheese until soft; blend in sour cream until smooth. Add mayonnaise, cream and salt to taste. Spoon dressing over each salad. Dust with paprika.

SERVES: 6 to 8

Seasonal samplings from Jr. League of Chicago

Three Bean Salad

Submitted by Mertie B. Ivory
Petersburg, Virginia

INGREDIENTS:

1 15-ounce can green beans
1 15-ounce can yellow wax beans
1 15-ounce can red kidney beans
1 medium size onion, chopped

1 cup sugar
½ cup white vinegar
½ cup olive oil

Drain and combine green beans, yellow wax and red kidney beans. Add chopped onions, sugar, white vinegar and olive oil to green beans, yellow wax and red kidney beans. Mix well. Let stand overnight in refrigerator before serving.

SERVES: 8 to 10

Ye Olde Sussex Sampler Cookbook

Perfect Caesar Salad

Submitted by Karen Shea
Richmond, Virginia

INGREDIENTS:

Romaine lettuce (enough for 4 people)
⅓ cup safflower or extra-dry virgin
    olive oil
¼ teaspoon salt and pepper
1 teaspoon grey poupon mustard
½ teaspoon Worcestershire sauce
8 dashes Tabasco sauce

2 tablespoons red wine vinegar
Juice of ½ lemon
1 egg equivalent (Egg Beaters)
3 cloves garlic, crushed
½ cup Parmesan cheese (from can)
1 tablespoon anchovy paste (optional)
Croutons

Cut up lettuce and set aside. Combine all other ingredients and toss over lettuce. Add croutons at serving time.

Note: Dressing can be prepared ahead and refrigerated. Toss with lettuce when ready to serve.

SERVES: 4

Family recipe

Broccoli Salad

Submitted by Tressie Smith
St. Albans, West Virginia

INGREDIENTS:

1 large bunch broccoli, chopped
½ cup pecans
½ cup onions, chopped

½ cup bacon bits
½ cup celery
½ cup raisons

INGREDIENTS: DRESSING

1 cup mayonnaise
¼ cup vinegar

½ cup sugar

Mix all together with Dressing: mayonnaise, sugar and vinegar.

SERVES: 6 to 8

Source unknown

Crab Salad

Submitted by Mary Ruth Anneren
Osprey, Florida

INGREDIENTS:

1 pound crabmeat
1 cup thin sliced celery
2 tablespoons Durkees Famous Sauce
⅓ cup mayonnaise

Dash of Worcestershire
1 tablespoon finely chopped onion
2 teaspoons lemon juice (or to taste)

Blend all ingredients, chill. Serve on salad greens and garnish.

Note: Can be used as a spread on crackers for an appetizer.

SERVES: 4 to 5

Original recipe

Colorful Ham-And-Rice Salad

Submitted by Jennie Fritz
Virginia Beach, Virginia

INGREDIENTS:

1 cup long grain rice, uncooked
1 (10 ounce) package frozen peas, thawed
    and drained
1 cup cooked ham, chopped
4 ounces Swiss cheese, chopped
¾ cup mayonnaise

½ cup chopped dill pickle
¼ cup chopped onion
½ teaspoon dried dill weed
½ teaspoon salt
¼ teaspoon pepper

Cook rice according to package directions, omitting salt: cool. Combine rice and the rest of the ingredients, stirring until mixed. Cover and chill thoroughly. Serve on lettuce leaves and garnish with tomato wedges, if desired.

SERVES: 6

Adapted from *Southern Living* Magazine

Apricot Salad

Submitted by Carol Mills
Ashland, Virginia

1 6-ounce package Apricot Jello
1 8-ounce package cream cheese, softened
1 20-ounce can crushed pineapple
    (undrained)

2 cups water (divided)
½ cup sugar
1 envelope of Dream Whip, prepared
    according to directions

INGREDIENTS:

Mix sugar, 1 cup water and undrained pineapple together in a saucepan. Cook over low heat and simmer a few minutes until it boils. Then add Jello. Remove from heat. Whip softened cream cheese into mixture. Add the other cup of water. Place in refrigerator until it begins to congeal, then fold in prepared Dream Whip. Pour into a shallow 8″×8″ dish and return to refrigerator until it sets.

SERVES: 8

Family recipe

Golden Glow Salad

Submitted by Carolyn Cottrell
Wicomico Church, Virginia

INGREDIENTS:

1 3-ounce package lemon or orange Jello
1 cup boiling water
1 cup canned pineapple juice
1 tablespoon vinegar or lemon juice
½ teaspoon salt (optional)

1 cup canned pineapple, diced and
   drained
1 cup grated raw carrots
⅓ cup pecans, finely cut
Crisp lettuce

Dissolve Jello in boiling water. Add pineapple juice (may have to add a little orange juice to make 1 cup) vinegar (or lemon juice) and salt. Chill. When slightly thickened, add pineapple, carrots and nuts. Turn into individual molds or 1-quart mold. Chill until firm. Unmold on lettuce. Garnish with mayonnaise.

SERVES: 6

Heavenly Orange Fluff Salad

Submitted by Mamie Sink
Chester, Virginia

INGREDIENTS:

2 3-ounce packages orange Jello
2 cups hot water
1 6-ounce can frozen orange juice
   concentrate, undiluted

2 cans (11 ounce) mandarin oranges,
   drained
1 8¼-ounce can crushed pineapple, not
   drained

Mix Jello with hot water. Stir in orange juice. Let cool. Add oranges and pineapple. Pour into 13 × 9 × 2-inch dish. Chill until set.

INGREDIENTS: TOPPING

1 package (3.4 ounce) instant lemon
   pudding

1 cup milk
½ cup sour cream

Mix milk with lemon pudding and beat 1 minute. Whip sour cream into pudding and spread on jello.

SERVES: 12

Easy Cranberry Salad

Submitted by Tressie Smith
St. Albans, West Virginia

INGREDIENTS:

2 packages strawberry gelatin
4 cups boiling water
1 can whole cranberry sauce

1 small can crushed pineapple, drained
½ cup chopped pecans
4 Golden Delicious apples, diced or grated

Dissolve gelatin in boiling water. Mash cranberry sauce and add to gelatin. Cool and add pineapple, pecans and apples. Pour into large mold and refrigerate.

SERVES: 12 or more

Source unknown

Cranberry Salad

Submitted by Jean W. Waymack
Prince George, Virginia

INGREDIENTS: SALAD

1 6-ounce box raspberry Jello
1½ cups boiling water
1 16-ounce can whole berry cranberry
    sauce

1 8-ounce can crushed pineapple
½ cup chopped celery
½ cup chopped pecans

Dissolve Jello in boiling water. Fold in cranberry sauce, pineapple, celery and nuts. Chill until firm. Use a Pyrex dish approximately 12 × 8.

INGREDIENTS: TOPPING

½ pint sour cream
1 8-ounce package cream cheese

¼ cup sugar
1 teaspoon vanilla

Whip sour cream and cream cheese together. Add sugar and vanilla. Spread on salad and top with finely chopped pecans.

Delicious salad for Thanksgiving or Christmas.

SERVES: 15 to 18

Family recipe

Corn Salad

Submitted by Christine Pitts
Hanover, Virginia

INGREDIENTS:

1 can corn, drained
1 can black beans, drained and rinsed
½ cup chopped green and red peppers
   combined
½ cup green onions
½ cup chopped celery

2 quartered tomatoes
1 tablespoon lemon juice
1 teaspoon chopped minced garlic
2 tablespoons olive oil
½–¾ cup picante sauce, mild to hot

Mix all ingredients together and marinate for 8 hours.

SERVES: 6–8

Family recipe

Marinated Cabbage Slaw

Submitted by Madelynne Chubin
Glen Allen, Virginia

INGREDIENTS: SLAW

1 16-ounce package shredded cabbage
   with carrots

or 1 small head cabbage, shredded and 2
   carrots, grated

INGREDIENTS: DRESSING

¾ cup cider vinegar
¼ cup water
1 teaspoon salt

½ teaspoon mustard seed
½ teaspoon celery seed
9 packets Sweet & Low sugar replacement

Combine vinegar, water, salt, mustard seed, celery seed and Sweet & Low in blender until well blended and Sweet & Low is dissolved. Pour over cabbage and carrots, mix thoroughly until well coated. Refrigerate at least 2 hours. Serve cold.

SERVES: 8

Original

Sig's Salad

Submitted by Sigrid Whittle
Richmond, Virginia

INGREDIENTS:

Romaine lettuce leaves
Sun dried tomatoes or fresh tomato slices
Crumbled Gorgonzola cheese
Toasted pine nuts

Salt and pepper to taste
Fresh basil or parsley, chopped
Olive oil
Balsamic vinegar

Arrange lettuce and tomatoes on individual salad plates. Sprinkle with Gorgonzola cheese, pine nuts, basil or parsley. Drizzle with olive oil and balsamic vinegar.

Note: No amounts are specified. You decide proportions. Delicious!

Original recipe

Orzo Salad

Submitted by Kathie Markel
Richmond, Virginia

INGREDIENTS:

1 pound orzo
1 bunch fresh parsley
1 bunch spring onions, white part plus
    some green
1 cup sliced black olives, drained

1 package crumbled feta cheese
1 package grape tomatoes (1 pint)
Bottle balsamic vinegar salad dressing
2 to 3 drops Tabasco

Cook orzo in boiling water until done. Drain. Wash parsley, cut off stems. Chop leafy part. Chop spring onions. Drain olives and discard liquid. Add all ingredients to orzo except dressing. To a small amount of dressing, add 2 to 3 squirts of Tabasco. Pour over orzo. Add more dressing to get to desired moisture. Up to ¾ cup.

Serve at room temperature or cold.

SERVES: 10

Family recipe

Tomato Aspic

Submitted by Shirley Olsson
Richmond, Virginia

INGREDIENTS:

1 large can tomatoes
3 cups tomato or V8 juice
2 onions, quartered
1 heaping tablespoon brown sugar
1 tablespoon vinegar
1 teaspoon pickling spice
8–10 drops Tabasco sauce
1–2 dashes Worcestershire sauce
Salt to taste

White pepper to taste
1–2 envelopes Knox Gelatin
¼–½ cup water
¾ cup coarse chopped green bell pepper,
 optional
¾ cup coarse chopped cucumber, optional
10–12 leaves of Boston butter lettuce
Real mayonnaise

Combine tomatoes, juice, onion, brown sugar, vinegar, pickling spice, Tabasco, Worcestershire, salt and pepper in a large pot. Boil until the onions are cooked. Strain and measure liquid.

While tomato mixture is cooking, soften gelatin in ¼ cup water per package. Use one envelop of gelatin for every 2 cups of final liquid. Add gelatin to tomato liquid. Add green pepper and/or cucumber if desired.

Grease individual molds with olive oil. Divide liquid among molds and refrigerate. Chill until firm. To serve, remove aspic from molds by briefly dipping bottom of molds in warm water. Place lettuce leaves on individual plates, unmold aspic on lettuce. Top with a dollop of mayonnaise.

SERVES: 10 to 12

Family recipe

Shrimp and White Bean Salad

Submitted by Hannah Gallier
Richmond, Virginia

INGREDIENTS:

2 19-ounce cans cannellini beans or other white beans, rinsed in a colander and drained well (about 4 cups)
1½ cups thinly sliced celery
½ cup thinly sliced red onions
1¼ pounds (about 36) shrimp, shelled and deveined (can use pre-cooked shrimp)
1 tablespoon minced garlic

¼ teaspoon dried hot red pepper flakes
6 tablespoons olive oil
¼ cup fresh lemon juice
¼ cup minced fresh parsley leaves
1 tablespoon fresh oregano leaves or 1 teaspoon crumbled dried plus, fresh oregano sprigs for garnish
8 lettuce leaves for lining the plates

In a bowl toss together gently the beans, celery, and onion. Reserve 8 whole shrimp for garnish, cut the remaining shrimp into thirds. In a large heavy skillet cook the garlic and the red pepper flakes in 3 tablespoons of the oil over moderate heat, stirring for 30 seconds, or until the garlic is very fragrant, add the shrimp (both the reserved and the cut shrimp), and cook the mixture, stirring for 2 to 3 minutes or until the shrimp are just cooked through. If you are using cooked shrimp, cook only until it has had time to absorb some of the flavor from the garlic and oil mixture. Transfer the whole shrimp to a bowl for garnish. Add the remaining shrimp mixture to the bean mixture. Drizzle the salad mixture with the lemon juice and the remaining 3 tablespoons oil, sprinkle it with the parsley, the minced oregano, and salt and pepper to taste, and toss it well. Arrange 2 of the lettuce leaves on each of four plates, divide the salad among the plates and garnish each serving with 2 of the whole shrimp and oregano sprigs.

SERVES: 4

Adapted from *Gourmet* Magazine

Pickled Cucumbers

Submitted by Babs Jackson
Richmond, Virginia

INGREDIENTS:

3 cucumbers, peeled and sliced thin
½ onion, sliced extremely thin
Salt, small amount (see Directions)
1 tablespoon wine vinegar or tarragon
vinegar

1 teaspoon sugar (approximately)
½ cup water
1 tablespoon (or more) mayonnaise or
salad dressing

Place cucumbers in shallow bowl and sprinkle *lightly* with salt. Add onion.

Combine in a jar wine or tarragon vinegar, sugar, water, mayonnaise or salad dressing. Cap the jar and shake well. Taste and adjust if necessary. Pour over cucumber mixture and marinate several hours, overnight or more.

SERVES: 6

Family recipe

Spinach Salad

Submitted by Babs Jackson,
President/CEO, HHH
Richmond, Virginia

SALAD INGREDIENTS:

10 ounces fresh spinach, washed and torn
1 cup fresh bean sprouts
½ 8-ounce can sliced water chestnuts

2 hard boiled eggs, chopped
6 slices bacon, cooked and crumbled
1 2-ounce jar pimentos, drained

DRESSING INGREDIENTS:

1 cup salad oil
¼ cup red wine vinegar
⅔ cup sugar
⅓ cup ketchup

1 medium onion, grated
2 teaspoons Worcestershire sauce
½ teaspoon salt

Gently toss salad ingredients together. Blend dressing in blender. Add about ½ cup dressing just before serving. Store remaining dressing in refrigerator.

SERVES: 4 to 6

Friend — Barbara Oakley

Baby Blue Salad

Submitted by Shelly Daffron
Richmond, Virginia

INGREDIENTS:

¾ pound mixed greens (Spring Mix)
4 ounces blue cheese, crumbled
1 pint blueberries

1 pint fresh strawberries
Balsamic vinaigrette (recipe follows)
Sweet and Spicy Pecans (recipe follows)

Assemble all salad ingredients. Toss with dressing. Sprinkle pecans on top.

INGREDIENTS: BALSAMIC VINAIGRETTE DRESSING

½ cup balsamic vinegar
3 tablespoons dijon mustard
3 tablespoons honey
2 cloves garlic, minced

¼ teaspoon salt
¼ teaspoon pepper
1 cup olive oil

Whisk together first 7 ingredients until blended. Gradually whisk in olive oil.

INGREDIENTS: SWEET AND SPICY PECANS

¼ cup sugar
1 cup warm water
1 cup pecan halves

2 tablespoons sugar
1 teaspoon chili powder
⅛ teaspoon ground red pepper

Stir together ¼ sugar and warm water until sugar dissolves. Add pecans, soak 10 minutes. Drain, discarding syrup.

Combine 2 tablespoons sugar, chili powder and ground red pepper.

Add pecans tossing to coat. Place pecans on lightly greased baking sheet.

Bake at 350° F for 10 minutes.

SERVES: 4

Family recipe

Chinese Cabbage Salad

Submitted by Marguerite Lawrence
Auroro, Colorado

INGREDIENTS:

1 large head Chinese (or Napa) cabbage
5–7 green onions
½ cup butter or margarine

2 packages Ramen soup noodles
¼ cup sesame seeds
1 2-ounce package chopped almonds

Chop Napa cabbage and green onions thinly. Mix well and refrigerate. Prepare "crunchies": in butter, brown noodles, almonds, and sesame seeds. Drain well on paper towels for at least 1 hour.

DRESSING INGREDIENTS:

1 cup vegetable oil
⅓ cup sugar

3 tablespoons soy sauce
4 tablespoons vinegar

Prepare Dressing: Mix oil, sugar, soy sauce, and vinegar in blender. Add "crunchies" and dressing to cabbage and onions at least ½ hour before serving. Mix well

SERVES: 6

Family recipe

Gran's Easy Tomato Aspic

Submitted by Nancy G. Powell
Richmond, Virginia

INGREDIENTS:

4 cups tomato juice
¼ cup water
2 small packages lemon jello
2 tablespoons horseradish
Shrimp, optional

1 envelope plain gelatin
1 teaspoon salt
1 tablespoon grated onion
1 tablespoon vinegar

Heat tomato juice and pour over lemon jello, stir to dissolve. Dissolve gelatin in ¼ cup water; add remaining ingredients. Pour into ring mold and refrigerate until set. To serve, fill center with cold, boiled shrimp if desired.

SERVES: 8 to 10

Neighbor—Helsee Gaddis

Tropical Spinach Salad with Homemade Cooked Dressing

Submitted by Deane R. Dubansky
Richmond, Virginia

INGREDIENTS:

5 cups torn fresh spinach
3 cups torn romaine lettuce
2 cups torn leaf lettuce
1 (11 ounce) can mandarin oranges,
  drained

1 small red onion, sliced very thinly and
  separated into rings
Cooked salad dressing (see below)
¼ cup toasted almonds (optional)

Place spinach, lettuces, oranges and onion in a large bowl. Toss with Cooked Salad Dressing. Sprinkle almonds, (if desired) over top. Serve immediately.

INGREDIENTS: COOKED SALAD DRESSING

¼ cup sugar
¼ cup white vinegar
¼ teaspoon salt
¼ teaspoon dry mustard

¼ teaspoon instant minced onion
Dash of paprika
1 egg, slightly beaten
¼ cup vegetable oil

Combine the sugar, white vinegar, salt, dry mustard, minced onion, paprika, and slightly beaten egg in a small saucepan and bring to a boil. Boil 1 minute. Gradually stir in the oil. Chill before dressing the salad.

Note: So delicious. Have copies of this recipe ready for your guests. They will want it.

YIELD: ¾ cup
SERVES: about 6

Family recipe

Potato Salad

Submitted by Elizabeth Jordan
Gloucester Point, Virginia

INGREDIENTS:

10–12 medium Red Bliss potatoes
    (approximately 5 pound bag
2 tablespoons minced onion
1 cup finely chopped celery
2 dill pickles, chopped
4 tablespoons dried parsley
12–15 strips bacon, cooked and broken
    into small pieces

2 teaspoons salt
½ teaspoon pepper
3 tablespoons vinegar
½ cup oil
2–2½ cups mayonnaise

Cook potatoes in salted water 30 to 40 minutes. Cool completely in refrigerator. Peel and cut into bite size pieces. Add onion, celery, pickles, parsley and bacon. Sprinkle with salt, pepper. Add combined vinegar and oil. Gently turn with wooden spoon. Add mayonnaise and turn again. Refrigerate several hours.

SERVES: 12 to 14

Family recipe

Pasta Salad

Submitted by Jo Ann Troy
Richmond, Virginia

INGREDIENTS:

16 ounces vermicelli
8 tablespoons salad oil
3 tablespoons lemon juice
1 tablespoon Accent
1 cup chopped celery
½ cup chopped onion

1 jar chopped pimento
1 chopped green pepper
1 can sliced ripe olives
1 pint mayonnaise
Salt to taste

Cook pasta and marinate overnight in salad oil, lemon juice and Accent. Add remaining ingredients and mix well.
Note: This is a pasta salad that even men enjoy.

SERVES: approximately 15

Family recipe

Shrimp Salad on Croissants
(Called "Seattle Special")

Submitted by Jane Whitaker
Richmond, Virginia

INGREDIENTS:

2 eggs, hard boiled and chopped
1 pound of shrimp, shelled and deveined
1 medium size ripe avocado, chopped

4 croissants, split in half
Lettuce

INGREDIENTS: SAUCE

⅔ cup mayonnaise
2 tablespoons chili sauce
1 tablespoon green onion, chopped (a bit less ok)

2 teaspoons Worcestershire sauce
2 teaspoons red wine vinegar
¼ teaspoon salt
⅛ teaspoon pepper

Combine all sauce ingredients, set aside.

In 3-quart saucepan over high heat, bring 2 inches of water to boiling. Add shrimp, heat to boiling again. Then, reduce heat to low and cook shrimp 1 minute or until tender; drain. Dice shrimp.

Mix sauce combo with shrimp, avocado and eggs. Place salad and lettuce on croissants.

SERVES: 4

Source unknown

Raisel's Chinese Chicken Salad

Submitted by Marsha Ginther
Midlothian, Virginia

INGREDIENTS:

¾ pound cooked chicken breasts, shredded
2 ounces crunchy chow mein noodles
1 head lettuce, shredded

1 can water chestnuts, sliced
2 tablespoons sesame seeds
¼ cup green onions, chopped

INGREDIENTS: DRESSING

2 tablespoons sugar
1 teaspoon salt
½ teaspoon pepper

¼ cup salad oil
3 tablespoons vinegar

Mix dressing and chill. Toss chicken with all remaining ingredients. Add dressing just before serving. Great way to use leftover chicken.

SERVES: 4

Family recipe

Chicken Salad

Submitted by Gay Cauthorn
Ashland, Virginia

INGREDIENTS:

Four boneless chicken breasts
Chicken broth to cover
1 cup chopped celery

1 tablespoon (fresh) lemon juice
½ cup (Dukes) mayonnaise
Salt and pepper to taste

Cook chicken breasts (boneless) until done (very tender). Cool in broth (can sit overnight in refrigerator in broth).

Cut into small pieces after cooling to make 2 cups. Toss in chopped celery. Add fresh lemon juice. Mix in Dukes mayonnaise. Add salt and pepper to taste.

Serve on crackers or sandwiches or on bed of lettuce.

SERVES: 5

Family recipe

Chicken Surprise

Submitted by Orlene S. James
Mt. Solon, Virginia

INGREDIENTS: DRESSING

2 tablespoons vegetable oil
2 tablespoons apple or white vinegar
2 tablespoons fine-chopped onion

1½ teaspoons salt
1 teaspoon curry powder
Dash pepper

Combine oil, vinegar, onions, salt, curry powder and pepper with a whisk, to make a dressing. Set aside.
Combine rice and chicken (or turkey), then add the celery and green pepper. Add mayonnaise and combine thoroughly.

INGREDIENTS: CHICKEN SALAD

1½ cups cold, cooked rice
2½ cups cold, cubed chicken (about 3
    breasts) (or turkey)
1 cup chopped celery

2 tablespoons fine-chopped green bell
    pepper
¾ cup mayonnaise

Pour dressing over the chicken mixture and combine thoroughly. Can be served by itself or stuffed into tomatoes. Best if allowed to sit for several hours in refrigerator.

SERVES: 6 to 8

Family recipe

Mixed Greens with Peanut Dressing

Submitted by Joyce Hughes
Richmond, Virginia

INGREDIENTS: DRESSING

3 tablespoons lite soy sauce
2 tablespoons chunky peanut butter
¼ cup vegetable oil

2 tablespoons white vinegar
1 tablespoon sugar

INGREDIENTS: SALAD

1 10-ounce package mixed salad greens
Purple onion, thinly sliced

1 red bell pepper, cut into thin strips

Whisk together soy sauce, peanut butter, vegetable oil, vinegar and sugar. Toss with greens, onions and pepper.

SERVES: 6

Adapted from *Southern Living* Magazine

Poppy Seed Dressing

Submitted by Grace W. Bailey
Richmond, Virginia

INGREDIENTS:

3 tablespoons cider vinegar
3 tablespoons sugar
½ teaspoon dry mustard

½ teaspoon salt
6 tablespoons vegetable oil
1 teaspoon poppy seeds

In small bowl or in blender beat or blend vinegar, sugar, mustard and salt 1 to 2 minutes. Gradually add oil a little at a time, beating until thick. Chill.

YIELDS: ⅔ cup

Newspaper recipe

Raspberry Balsamic Dressing

Submitted by Maria Romhilt
Richmond, Virginia

INGREDIENTS:

1 12-ounce bag frozen raspberries,
  well thawed
¼ cup sugar
¼ cup shallot flavored vinegar
¼ cup balsamic vinegar

1½ tablespoon dijon mustard
½ teaspoon salt
1 teaspoon lemon juice
1 cup olive oil

Puree berries in blender and put through coarse sieve to remove seeds. Put pureed berries in blender and add sugar, vinegars, mustard, salt, lemon juice and pulse after each addition. Add oil slowly while running blender. Store dressing in refrigerator.

Serving suggestion: Drizzle over field greens or arugula and add crumbled goat cheese.

YIELDS: about 2 cups dressing

Adapted from *Bon Appetit*

Quick Hollandaise Sauce

Submitted by Barbara T. Lester, M.D.
Richmond, Virginia

INGREDIENTS:

4 tablespoons mayonnaise
2 teaspoons prepared mustard

1 teaspoon lemon juice
1 tablespoon melted butter

Mix mayonnaise, mustard, lemon juice and butter together with a fork in a small frying pan. Heat slowly to prevent curdling. Serve over your choice of vegetables. Broccoli or asparagus are good choices.

SERVES: 4 to 6

Friend — Jerrie Thornton

Marinade for Steak or Chicken

Submitted by Patty Giles
Richmond, Virginia

INGREDIENTS:

½ cup soy sauce
¼ cup oil (vegetable oil)
2 tablespoons brown sugar

2 teaspoons ground ginger
2 teaspoons dry mustard
3 teaspoons minced garlic

Mix soy sauce, vegetable oil, brown sugar, ginger, dry mustard and garlic. Pour over chicken pieces (or steaks). Refrigerate until ready to put on grill.

YIELDS: enough for 4 to 6 pieces chicken or steak

Family recipe

Bleu Cheese Walnut Butter

Submitted by Maria Romhilt
Richmond, Virginia

INGREDIENTS:

1 container Land o Lakes Whipped
   Light Butter

4 ounces crumbled bleu cheese
¼ cup walnuts, finely ground

Soften bleu cheese and butter to room temperature. Beat with mixer until well blended. Mix in nuts well. Store in freezer. Use on grilled steaks or fish. Remove from freezer and bring to room temperature before putting on grilled steak or fish hot off the grill

SERVES: Varies

Original recipe

Marinade for Game Hens or Turkey Breast

Submitted by Kathie Markel
Richmond, Virginia

INGREDIENTS:

6 cloves garlic
⅓ cup fresh lime juice
⅓ cup rice wine or dry sherry
1 tablespoon Asian chili sauce
1 cup chopped mixed basil, cilantro
    and mint
2 tablespoons fresh ginger, chopped

⅓ cup olive oil
¼ cup soy sauce
¼ cup chopped parsley
Zest from 2 limes, chopped
⅓ cup hoison sauce
2 tablespoons honey
2 green onions, chopped

Mix all ingredients together and pour over poultry in plastic bag to marinate. Grill or roast, baste during cooking.

YIELD: About 2½ cups marinade

Adapted from *Hot Barbecue Cookbook*

Eggs and Cheese

Janet's Pineapple Casserole

Submitted by Nancy G. Powell
Richmond, Virginia

INGREDIENTS:

3 well-beaten eggs
½ cup sugar + 1 tablespoon
1.5 pound can crushed pineapple,
    undrained

½ cup cheddar cheese, grated (optional)
1 tablespoon flour
3 slices white bread, cubed
1 stick margarine, melted

Combine eggs, sugar and flour; stir in pineapple. Pour into casserole. Top with bread cubes. Pour melted butter over bread. Bake at 350° F for 45 minutes, or until golden brown. Sprinkle cheese on top and return to oven just until cheese begins to melt.

This may be served as a side dish, or as a light dessert.

SERVES: 6

Friend — Janet Fuller

French Toast

Submitted by Patty Giles
Richmond, Virginia

INGREDIENTS:

6 eggs
⅔ cup orange juice
⅓ cup Grand Marnier
⅓ cup milk
3 tablespoons sugar
¼ teaspoon vanilla
¼ teaspoon salt

1 teaspoon grated orange peel
8–10 slices French bread (or wheat slices)
3–4 tablespoons butter
Powdered sugar
Butter
Maple syrup

Beat eggs in large bowl. Add milk, sugar, orange juice, Grand Marnier, vanilla, salt and orange peel. Mix well. Melt butter in large skillet over medium high heat. Dip bread into egg mixture and cook until browned. Turn and continue cooking. Cut bread diagonally, arrange on platter and sprinkle with powdered sugar. Serve immediately with butter and maple syrup.

SERVES: 4 or 5

Friend Eleanor's recipe

Egg Casserole

Submitted by Clara Bray
Reedville, Virginia

INGREDIENTS:

30 saltine crackers, crumbled
6 eggs, slightly beaten
6 strips bacon, cooked and crumbled

2 cups milk
2 cups shredded cheese
¼ cup butter or margarine

Put crackers in greased 11×7 baking dish. Combine remaining ingredients; pour over crackers. Cover and refrigerate overnight. Remove from refrigerator 30 minutes before baking. Bake, uncovered, at 325° F for 45 minutes. Let stand 5 minutes before cutting.

SERVES: 8

Family recipe

French Toast Casserole

Submitted by Annette Gelber
Richmond, Virginia

INGREDIENTS:

1 10-ounce French or Italian loaf
8 eggs
3 cups whole milk
6 teaspoons sugar

¾ teaspoon salt
1 tablespoon vanilla extract
½ teaspoon cinnamon
2 tablespoons butter, slivered

Lightly grease 9 × 13 inch baking pan. Slice bread 1-inch thick and place in single layer in bottom of pan.

In large bowl, beat eggs, milk, salt, vanilla and cinnamon. Pour over bread slices, cover and refrigerate overnight.

In the morning, uncover and let stand at room temperature while oven pre-heats to 350°. Dot with butter slivers and bake until puffy and light brown, about 40 minutes. Let stand 5 minutes. Serve with chilled fresh fruit, maple syrup, honey or yogurt.

SERVES: 8

Newspaper recipe

Nacho Casserole

Submitted by Marion Badenoch
Reedville, Virginia

INGREDIENTS:

1 can cheddar cheese soup (undiluted)
½ cup milk
1 16-ounce jar medium salsa
1 7-ounce bag tortilla chips

1 16-ounce can fat free refried beans
1 cup shredded cheddar cheese
1 or 2 sliced jalapeno chilies

Mix soup and milk and spread evenly on bottom of 9″ × 13″ glass baking dish. Top with ½ the salsa and ½ the tortilla chips. Spread carefully with refried beans. Top with remaining chips and salsa. Sprinkle with shredded cheese and jalapenos. Bake at 400° F for 20 minutes until heated through. Freezes well.

SERVES: 8

Family recipe

Brunch Casserole

Submitted by Kathy Burns
Richmond, Virginia

INGREDIENTS:

8 slices bread (trim crust—staler bread
    better)
1 pound grated sharp cheddar cheese
1 pound cooked sausage (not dry)
3 or 4 eggs

2 cups milk
½ teaspoon salt
1 teaspoon dry mustard
Dash pepper

Grease 9×13 dish, line with bread on bottom, then cheese, then sausage. Mix eggs, milk and seasonings. Pour mixture into pan, refrigerate overnight. Bake at 350° F for 30 to 35 minutes.

This is very good and easy!

You can also add chopped onions and green peppers for a little extra flavor and texture.

SERVES: 8

Source unknown

Breakfast Tomorrow

Submitted by Joyce Crostic
Midlothian, Virginia

INGREDIENTS:

14–15 slices of day-old bread (cubed)
1 pound sausage
2 cups shredded cheddar cheese
6 eggs

1 teaspoon salt
½ teaspoon pepper
1 tablespoon mustard
3 cups milk

Line the bottom of 9×12 baking dish with cubes of bread. Saute sausage, drain. Pour sausage over bread cubes. Spread cheddar cheese over sausage. Beat eggs, milk, salt, pepper, and mustard together. Pour gently over sausage mixture in baking dish. Seal tightly with foil or plastic wrap. Refrigerate at least 24 hours. Bake uncovered at 350° F for 1 hour or until light brown.

SERVES: 10

Source unknown

Elegant Crab Brunch Bake

Submitted by Cathy B. Hinton
Midlothian, Virginia

INGREDIENTS:

1½ cups unseasoned croutons
¼ cup butter or margarine, melted
8 ounces crabmeat
2 teaspoons Sauer's Chesapeake Seafood
    Seasoning
¼ cup sliced green onions

2 teaspoons Sauer's Parsley Flakes
1 cup (4 ounces) shredded Cheddar cheese
3 eggs, beaten
1½ cups milk
½ cup dairy sour cream
½ teaspoon Sauer's Dry Mustard

Butter an 8-inch square baking dish. Place half of the croutons in dish; drizzle with half of butter. Layer with half of the crabmeat, Seafood Seasoning, green onions, parsley and cheese. Repeat layers. Beat together remaining ingredients. Pour over layers; sprinkle with additional Seafood Seasoning. Cover; refrigerate overnight. Let stand at room temperature while preheating oven to 350° F. Uncover and bake 35 minutes or until puffed and golden. Let stand 10 minutes before serving.

SERVES: 6

Original recipe

David Ayers Pancake

Submitted by Richard Bragg
Richmond, Virginia

INGREDIENTS:

2 beaten eggs
½ cup plain flour
½ cup milk
Pinch of nutmeg

½ stick of butter, melted
Confectioner's sugar
Honey/Lemons

Preheat oven to 400° F. Grease non-metallic 9 by 15 baking dish with butter. Combine eggs, flour, milk, nutmeg and melted butter. Pour into baking dish. Bake for 15 minutes. Cut into 4 pieces, sprinkle confectioner's sugar on top, squirt fresh lemon on top, drizzle with honey.

SERVES: 2

Family recipe

Chakchouka (Pronounced Shakshouka)

Submitted by Teresa Banyas
Clarksville, Virginia

INGREDIENTS:

1 medium sliced onion
1 sliced green pepper
3 or 4 good size ripe tomatoes, chopped, or
    an equal amount canned with juice

6 to 8 eggs
½ pound bulk sausage, cooked and
    drained
Oil for frying (preferably olive)

On low flame, heat a 10-inch skillet, pour in oil to cover bottom. Add onion and pepper and sauté until softened. Add tomatoes, cover, and turn up heat until tomatoes release their juice and are steaming. Add cooked sausage, then gently break the eggs, one at a time, over mixture. Cover, lower heat and cook until eggs set. Cut in wedges and serve. Also good without sausage.

SERVES: 4

Source unknown (came from Tunisia, No. Africa)

Frittata

Submitted by Carol Jarett
Richmond, Virginia

INGREDIENTS:

1 cup thin sliced onion
⅓ cup olive oil
3 small zucchini, sliced paper thin
6 extra large eggs
½ teaspoon salt

½ teaspoon finely ground black pepper
5 tablespoons grated Parmesan cheese
4 tablespoons butter
1 tablespoon finely chopped parsley
1 or 2 basil leaves, thinly sliced

Cook onion in olive oil until transparent. Add zucchini and brown lightly. Reduce heat, cook for 5 minutes more, season with salt and pepper, drain and cool slightly. Beat eggs in bowl, add zucchini and onion mixture and 4 tablespoons of Parmesan cheese.

Heat butter over medium-low heat in heavy 10″ skillet, preferably cast iron, until it bubbles. Pour egg mixture into pan, add the parsley and basil. Keep heat very low, cook until eggs have set, about 20 minutes. Sprinkle with remaining Parmesan cheese, and put under hot broiler for about 1 minute, until top is set, but not brown. Run sharp knife around edges of frittata to loosen it from pan, slide it onto a large plate, and cool slightly. Cut in wedges, and serve.

This is equally delicious if you substitute other veggies and add meat, such as potatoes, cubed cooked ham, crisp cooked bacon pieces, etc. A good way to use leftover veggies.

SERVES: 6

The New James Beard Cookbook

No-Fail Cheese Souffle

Submitted by Nancy Konopelski
Richmond, Virginia

INGREDIENTS:

1 can cheddar cheese soup (undiluted)
½ cup milk
1 16-ounce jar medium salsa
1 7-ounce bag tortilla chips

1 16-ounce can fat free refried beans
1 cup shredded cheddar cheese
1 or 2 sliced jalapeno chilies

Dice cheese and set aside. Butter the dish. Separate the eggs.

In the top of a double boiler melt the butter and blend in flour and seasonings. Add milk all at once; cook until thick, stirring constantly. Add the cheese; cook until melted. Remove the double boiler pan from over the hot water. Beat egg whites until stiff but moist. Beat egg yolks until thick. Add yolks to the mixture; fold in egg whites and pour into buttered 2 quart dish. Oven—350° F. Bake time—50 minutes.

SERVES: 4

Breaking Bread Together Cookbook

Cheddar-Spinach Quiche

Submitted by Ann Bendheim
Richmond, Virginia

INGREDIENTS:

1½ cups unseasoned croutons
¼ cup butter or margarine, melted
8 ounces crabmeat
2 teaspoons Sauer's Chesapeake Seafood
    Seasoning
¼ cup sliced green onions

2 teaspoons Sauer's Parsley Flakes
1 cup (4 ounces) shredded Cheddar cheese
3 eggs, beaten
1½ cups milk
½ cup dairy sour cream
½ teaspoon Sauer's Dry Mustard

Cook spinach according to package direction, and drain well.

Toss the cheese and flour together.

Mix together cheese, spinach, milk, eggs, salt, and pepper. Pour mixture into the pastry shell. Bake in a 350° F oven for 1 hour.

SERVES: 4 to 6

Source unknown

Cheese Strata

Submitted by Babs Jackson,
President/CEO, HHH

INGREDIENTS:

12 slices white bread
¾ pound sharp processed American
    cheese, sliced
1 10-ounce package frozen chopped
    broccoli, cooked and drained
2 cups finely diced ham

6 slightly beaten eggs
3½ cups milk
2 tablespoons instant minced onion
½ teaspoon salt
¼ teaspoon dry mustard

Cut 12 rounds from bread, using a drinking glass. Set aside. Fit scraps of bread in bottom of greased 13×9×2 inch baking dish. Place cheese in layer over bread. Add a layer of broccoli, then ham. Arrange bread rounds on top. Combine eggs, milk, onion, salt and mustard and pour over bread and all. Cover and refrigerate overnight. Bake uncovered at 325°–350° F for 55 minutes. Sprinkle with shredded cheese last 5 minutes. Let stand 10 minutes before cutting.

YIELDS: 12 squares

Friend's recipe

Entrees

Mahi Mahi with Macadamia Nuts

Submitted by Babs Jackson,
President/CEO, HHH

INGREDIENTS:

1½ pounds fresh or frozen mahi mahi fillets
1 8¾-ounce can pineapple slices
1 tablespoon soy sauce
¼ teaspoon salt

Pepper to taste
½ teaspoon ground ginger
¼ cup chopped macadamia nuts

Remove skin and cut fillets into 4 portions. Drain pineapple and reserve ½ cup syrup. In small bowl, combine reserved syrup with soy sauce, salt and pepper. Place fish in single layer in shallow dish. Pour syrup mixture over fish and let stand at room temperature for 30 minutes, turning once. Drain and reserve the marinade. Place fish on greased broiler rack. Broil 4 inches from heat, until fillets flake easily with fork, about 10 minutes. Brush often with reserved marinade. During last few minutes of broiling, place pineapple slices on fillets. Brush with marinade and heat through. Sprinkle nuts on fish and pineapple slices.

SERVES: 4

Purple Sage — Junior League of Tucson, AZ (1986)

Tropical Chicken Livers

Submitted by Babs Jackson,
President/CEO, HHH

INGREDIENTS:

1½ pounds chicken livers
¼ teaspoon garlic powder
¼ cup flour
¼ teaspoon salt
¼ teaspoon pepper
½ cup oil
1 16-ounce can pineapple chunks

1 cup chopped celery
1 cup chopped scallion
½ cup chopped green bell pepper
½ pound mushrooms, sliced
8 water chestnuts, thinly sliced
3 tablespoons soy sauce
1 teaspoon ground ginger

Wash and thoroughly dry livers. Sprinkle with garlic powder and set aside for 1 hour. Dust livers with flour, salt and pepper. Sauté in oil for 3 minutes. Drain pineapple and reserve liquid. Add pineapple chunks to livers and brown slightly. Be careful not to overcook. Add celery, scallions, green pepper, mushrooms, water chestnuts, soy sauce and ginger. Cook about 5 minutes. Vegetables should remain crisp. Stir in 3 tablespoons reserved pineapple juice.

SERVES: 6 to 8

Source unknown

Pineapple Beef Stir-Fry

Submitted by Louis Mahoney
Richmond, Virginia

INGREDIENTS:

1 pound boneless top sirloin or tenderloin
   steak, cut into strips
½ cup steak sauce
1 tablespoon cornstarch
1 tablespoon vegetable oil

1 (8 ounce) can pineapple chunks,
   drained, reserving ⅓ cup juice
½ cup minced green onion or shallots
Hot cooked rice

Mix beef, steak sauce and cornstarch until well coated. Drain beef, reserving steak sauce mixture. Cook and stir beef strips in hot oil in large skillet or wok for 3 to 4 minutes. Add pineapple chunks, onion or shallots, reserved pineapple juice and steak sauce mixture. Heat to a boil. Reduce heat and simmer 1 minute. Serve over rice.

SERVES: 4

Adapted from iGourmet.com

Beef Tenderloin

Submitted by Cary Dabney
Richmond, Virginia

INGREDIENTS:

Whole beef tenderloin
Olive oil

Fresh garlic, slivered
Montreal Steak seasoning to taste

Rub lightly with olive oil on a whole beef tenderloin. Cut slits in it and put slivers of fresh garlic in the slits—about a dozen or so. Sprinkle generously all over with Montreal Steak Seasoning. Bring tenderloin to room temperature (very important). Bake uncovered at 400° F for 40 minutes. This turns out perfectly (medium to dark pink color) every time.

SERVES: 12+

Source unknown

Steak à la Patsy

Submitted by Annette Gelber
Richmond, Virginia

INGREDIENTS:

4 slices bacon, diced small
¼ cup olive oil
1 medium size onion, peeled and
    thinly sliced
4 scallions, thinly sliced
2 tablespoons chopped fresh basil

½ cup chicken broth
¼ cup dry white wine
½ teaspoon salt
¼ teaspoon freshly ground black pepper
2 sirloin steaks: 1¼ pounds each,
    thickness 1¼ inch

Heat broiler. Place large non-stick skillet over low heat. Add bacon and sauté until crisp, 4 to 5 minutes. Transfer to paper towels to drain; reserve.

Wipe pan, return to low heat, add oil and onion and saute until almost carmelized, about 10 minutes. Add reserved bacon, scallions, basil, broth, wine, salt and pepper. Bring to a boil, reduce heat to low and simmer until liquid is reduced by half, 2 to 3 minutes. Remove from heat and keep warm.

Place steaks in broiler about 3 inches from heat. Broil to taste, turning once. Transfer steaks to heated platter, pour sauce on top and serve.

SERVES: 4

Patsy's Italian Restaurant, New York City

Mom's Adjusted Brisket

Submitted by Madelynne Chubin
Glen Allen, Virginia

INGREDIENTS:

4–6 pound brisket
1 cup sliced carrots
1 medium onion, sliced
6–8 cloves garlic
2 cans Healthy Choice Cream of
    Mushroom Soup

1 cup dry red wine (optional)
1 cup brewed coffee
1 package onion soup mix
1–2 cups water
½ cup sliced mushrooms (optional)
Salt and pepper to taste

Place meat in covered roasting pan. Put onions, carrots, mushrooms and garlic around the meat. Cover with the canned and dry soup. Pour in liquids. Roast approximately 2 hours in 350° F oven. Cool, then refrigerate overnight. Before serving skim fat from top of gravy, then slice meat, return to gravy and cook on top of stove on low heat, about 1 hour. Thicken gravy if necessary.

SERVES: 8 to 10

Family recipe

1-2-3 Pot Roast

Submitted by Kate Yoffy
Richmond, Virginia

INGREDIENTS:

1 Reynolds oven cooking bag
¼ cup flour
1 2–4 pound boneless beef chuck roast
1–2 medium onions cut into chunks
    or slices

1 green pepper cut into chunks
carrots (as many as you like) peeled and
    cut into pieces
1 jar (16 ounce) chunky picante sauce or
    salsa, any brand or "hot" you prefer

Preheat your oven to 325° F.

Shake flour in the cooking bag. Place the bag on a large cookie pan with sides.

Place chuck roast in the cooking bag. Put the onions, green pepper, and carrots in the bag, on top and around the roast. Top with the picante sauce.

Close the bag with the tie provided and cut a small slit in the top of the bag according to package directions.

Bake roast until tender—anywhere between 2 to 3 hours depending on the size of roast.

SERVES: 4 to 6

Family recipe

West Coast Broiled Flank Steak

Submitted by Annette Gelber
Richmond, Virginia

INGREDIENTS:

1 flank steak, about 1½ pounds

1 onion, thinly sliced

1 teaspoon freshly grated lemon peel

½ cup fresh lemon juice

2 tablespoons sugar

½ teaspoon salt

½ teaspoon oregano, crushed

⅛ teaspoon coarse black pepper

2 tablespoons soy sauce

1 tablespoon butter

Trim any fat or membrane from steak. With knife, score steak ⅛ inch deep on both sides in diamond pattern. Layer half of onions in plastic bag or glass dish. Place steak on top of onions; cover with remaining onions. Thoroughly combine lemon peel, lemon juice, sugar, salt, oregano, black pepper and soy sauce (but no butter); pour over steak and onions; cover. Marinate 2 to 3 hours or overnight in refrigerator and turn several times.

Remove steak from marinade; wipe partially dry with paper towel. Drain onions and reserve. Place steak on cold broiler pan, 3 to 5 inches from source of heat in a pre-heated broiler. Broil 3 to 5 minutes on each side. Meanwhile, saute onions in the 1 tablespoon butter until soft. To serve, cut steak across grain in thin slices; top with onions.

SERVES: 4

Beef Stew

Submitted by Babs Jackson,
President and CEO

INGREDIENTS:

3–4 pounds stew meat

4 large carrots

4 potatoes

1½ cans tomato soup

1½ cans dry red wine

2 onions, quartered

1 teaspoon oregano

Salt and pepper to taste

Garlic salt to taste

½ package frozen peas

Mix all ingredients except peas together in an ovenproof pot. Cook covered for 5 hours in a 275° F oven. During last half-hour, add frozen peas.

SERVES: 6 to 8

Curtis' BBQ Sauce Meatloaf

Submitted by Debi Somerville
Fredericksburg, Virginia

LOAF INGREDIENTS:

2–3 pounds ground beef
2 eggs
1 cup bread crumbs, seasoned
4 ounces BBQ sauce
3 tablespoons dried or ½ cup fresh
    minced onions

2 tablespoons dried parsley
Dash of Worcestershire or hot sauce
Seasoning salt to taste
Salt and pepper to taste
1 small can mushrooms

Mix all together and form loaf. Place in loaf pan and bake at 325° F for 1½ hours and check with meat probe for doneness.

TOPPING INGREDIENTS:

BBQ sauce to coat
Cheese for melting (your choice)

When done, turn off oven. Coat with additional BBQ sauce and any melting cheese such as American, cheddar, Provolone, etc. Return to warm oven to melt cheese.

SERVES: 6 to 8

Original recipe—Curtis Somerville

Hawaiian Meat Balls

Submitted by Gerry Herring
Richmond, Virginia

INGREDIENTS:

1½ pounds LEAN ground beef
2 tablespoons minced green onions
2 tablespoons minced green pepper
½ teaspoon salt
1 tablespoon vegetable oil
1 teaspoon soy sauce

1 10¾ can tomato soup
⅓ cup water
½ cup crushed pineapple in unsweetened
    juice, drained
Dash ground ginger
Cooked noodles or rice, optional

Combine beef, onion, green pepper, and salt; mix well. Shape into 24 meat balls. Heat oil in a large frying pan. Brown meat balls over medium heat; drain fat. Add soup, water, pineapple, soy sauce and ginger. Cover and cook over low heat for 20 minutes. Stir occasionally.

SERVES: Many

Family recipe

Hamburger Corn Casserole

Submitted by Lynn Parker
Benson, North Carolina

INGREDIENTS:

1 pound hamburger
1 small onion (chopped)
2 small jars diced pimentos
1 10-ounce can cream of chicken soup
1 10-ounce can cream of mushroom soup

1 10-ounce can whole kernel corn
1 16-ounce sour cream
3 cups cooked egg noodles
8–10 slices white bread
1 stick margarine

In 10-inch skillet brown hamburger with onion until hamburger is no longer pink. Drain and place back into skillet. Add pimentos, cream of chicken, cream of mushroom soup, corn and sour cream. Cook on low heat until warm. Cook egg noodles by cooking directions on bag, then drain and pour into 13 × 9 inch pan. Pour hamburger mixture over noodles and mix well. Tear bread into small pieces and cover top of casserole, then pour melted margarine over bread. Place in 350° F oven until bread is toasted, 20 to 30 minutes.

SERVES: 4 to 5

Family recipe

Sloppy Joe

Submitted by Judy Jones
Midlothian, Virginia

INGREDIENTS:

1 pound lean ground chuck
½ teaspoon salt
¼ teaspoon pepper
¼ teaspoon sage
1 cup catsup
½ cup water (use less water particularly if
   making larger batch)

1 medium onion cut finely
½ teaspoon chili powder
1 tablespoon sugar
2 teaspoons Worcestershire sauce

Brown beef and onion together in large pot. Drain off any fat. Add remainder of ingredients. Stir together well; cook slowly; stir occasionally for about an hour. Cover pot if too much liquid is steaming away. Serve on toasted bun. Mixture freezes well.

SERVES: 5 average

Friend—Phyllis Christiansen

Meat Loaf

Submitted by Judy Jones
Midlothian, Virginia

MEAT LOAF INGREDIENTS:

1 pound ground chuck
1 slice bread torn into small pieces
1 medium onion, minced

1 large egg, beaten
½ cup tomato sauce
Salt and pepper to taste

Preheat oven to 350° F.

Mix together beef, bread pieces, onion, beaten egg, tomato sauce, salt and pepper. Form into loaf and place in a loaf pan.

SAUCE INGREDIENTS:

½ cup tomato sauce
1½ teaspoon salt
¼ teaspoon pepper
2 tablespoons vinegar

1 tablespoon Dijon mustard
¼ cup water
2 tablespoons brown sugar
1½ teaspoons Worcestershire sauce

Combine tomato sauce, salt, pepper, vinegar, mustard, water, brown sugar and Worcestershire sauce. Pour over meat.

Bake in oven uncovered for 1 hour, 15 minutes. Baste occasionally.

SERVES: 4 to 6

Pumpkin Stew/Carbonada Criolla

Submitted by Delegate Karen Darner
Arlington, Virginia

INGREDIENTS:

10–12 pound pumpkin or other large
    winter squash
½ cup butter (¼ pound stick) softened
1 cup sugar
2 tablespoons olive oil
2 pounds lean beef chuck, cut into
    1 inch cubes
1 cup coarsely chopped onions
½ cup coarsely chopped green pepper
½ teaspoon finely chopped garlic
4 cups fresh beef stock or 2 cups canned
    stock with 2 cups cold water
3 medium tomatoes, peeled, seeded and
    coarsely chopped or substitute 1
    cup chopped, drained, canned
    Italian plum tomatoes
½ teaspoon dried oregano

1 bay leaf
1 teaspoon salt
Freshly ground black pepper
1½ pounds sweet potatoes, peeled and cut
    into to inch cubes (about 4½ cups)
1½ pounds white potatoes, peeled and cut
    into ½ inch cubes (about 4½ cups)
½ pound zucchini, scrubbed but not
    peeled, and cut into ¼ inch slices
    (1½ cups)
3 ears corn, shucked and cut into rounds
    1 inch wide
4 fresh peaches, peeled, halved and pitted,
    or substitute 8 canned white peach
    halves, drained and rinsed in cold
    water

Preheat the oven to 375° F. Scrub outside of pumpkin under cold running water with a stiff brush. With a large, sharp knife, cut down into the top of pumpkin to create a lid 6–7 inches in diameter. Leave stem intact as a handle. Lift out lid and with a large metal spoon, scrape seeds and stringy fibers from lid and from pumpkin shell.

Brush inside of pumpkin with soft butter and sprinkle cup of sugar into the opening. Tip the pumpkin from side to side to make the sugar adhere to the butter. Then turn the pumpkin over and gently shake out excess sugar. Put the lid back in place.

Place the pumpkin in a large shallow roasting pan and bake in the oven 45 minutes or until tender but somewhat resistant when pierced with the tip of a small, sharp knife. The pumpkin shell should remain firm enough to hold the filling without danger of collapsing.

Meanwhile, heat oil over moderate heat in a heavy 6–8 quart casserole until a light haze forms above it. Add the cubes of meat and brown them on all sides, turning them frequently with a large spoon. Regulate heat so the meat browns quickly without burning. Then with a slotted spoon, transfer the meat to a platter.

To the fat remaining in the pan, add the onions, green pepper and garlic, and cook over moderate heat, stirring constantly, for about 5 minutes, or until the vegetables are soft but not brown. Pour in the fresh beef stock and bring to a boil over high heat, meanwhile scraping in any brown bits clinging to the bottom and sides of the pan. Return the meat and any of its accumulated juices to the pan and stir in the tomatoes, oregano, bay leaf, salt and a few grindings of black pepper. Cover the pan, reduce the heat to low, and simmer undisturbed for 15 minutes. Then add the sweet potatoes and white potatoes, cover the pan and cook for 15 minutes; add the zucchini slices, cover the pan again and cook for 10 minutes. Finally add the corn rounds and peach halves and cook, still covered, for 5 minutes longer.

Pour the entire content of the pan carefully into the baked pumpkin, cover the pumpkin with its lid again, and bake for another 15 minutes in a 375° F oven. To serve, place the pumpkin on a large serving platter and, at the table, ladle the *carbonada* from the pumpkin onto heated, individual serving plates.

Note: Can be adapted easily to be vegetarian.

SERVES: 6

Stuffed Veal Rolls

Submitted by Annette Gelber
Richmond, Virginia

INGREDIENTS:

12 thin slices veal, pounded
12 thin slices prosciutto
12 thin slices mozzarella
3 tablespoons dried basil or chopped fresh
    basil leaves
2 teaspoons chopped fresh sage
Freshly ground black pepper

4 tablespoons cream sherry
6 tablespoons clarified butter
½ cup dry white wine
6 teaspoons fresh lemon juice
2 teaspoons chopped fresh parsley leaves
Salt and freshly ground black pepper
6 lemon wedges for garnish

Lay veal slices on work surface. Place a slice of prosciutto and a slice of mozzarella on each. Sprinkle with a little basil, sage and black pepper. Roll up the veal tightly into cylinders and fasten with a toothpick.

Use a skillet large enough to place veal rolls in single layer. Heat it over high heat and pour the sherry into the hot pan, tipping it to coat the bottom evenly. Add the butter and, when hot, brown veal rolls completely. Add the white wine, lemon juice and parsley to the pan and season with salt and pepper to taste. Lower the heat and cook for 10 to 15 minutes. Transfer veal rolls to a warm serving dish and garnish with lemon wedges.

Note: To clarify butter, cut unsalted butter into small pieces and melt over low heat without stirring or allowing it to sizzle. Simmer 10 to 15 minutes. Strain well and let clear yellow mixture cool. Use only in cooking, not as a spread.

SERVES: 6

Family recipe

Butterflied Leg of Lamb

Submitted by Jane Whitaker
Richmond, Virginia

INGREDIENTS:

1 boneless leg of lamb (3 to 4 pounds)
    trimmed of visible fat and butterflied

MARINADE:

½ cup red current jelly, melted
½ cup freshly squeezed lemon juice
2 tablespoons olive oil
1½ tablespoons salt

4 teaspoons ground coriander seeds
4 or 5 small cloves of garlic, crushed
1 teaspoon fresh ground pepper

Mix marinade. Pour in heavy plastic bag and add meat. Refrigerate at least 8 hours, up to 2 days, turning several times. Remove meat and discard marinade. Grill 10 to 15 minutes per side depending on thickness. Can also be broiled.

SERVES: 8

Source unknown

Venison BBQ

Submitted by Steve Ault
Richmond, Virginia

INGREDIENTS:

Venison, any part
1 large onion
Season Salt

4 strips of thick sliced bacon
Heavy aluminum foil

Slice onion into thick pieces and place on meat, sprinkle season salt over both sides of meat, place 2 pieces of bacon on each side and wrap meat in foil about three times to seal meat tight. Place on low gas grill and turn every 15 minutes for about 2 hours. The meat does not have to be fully cooked. If you use briquettes, place meat off to the side so you won't burn the meat. Remove meat and let cool, shred (do not cut the meat) and place in a crock-pot, pour your favorite BBQ sauce over the meat and cook on low for 6 to 8 hours, if possible stir every hour.

Venison Stew

Submitted by Steve Ault
Richmond, Virginia

INGREDIENTS:

1 leg of Venison boned to fit your crock-
    pot or Dutch oven
2 large onions
1 small bag of mini carrots
1 to 2 pounds of mini red potatoes
    (any potato will do)

1 large container of fresh mushrooms
    (canned will do)
1 large bay leaf
Salt and pepper to taste
2 tablespoons of A-1 sauce
1 can of Rotel brand tomatoes
Optional ½ cup of sour cream

Place roast in crock pot or Dutch oven. Dice and add the 2 large onions. Add the bay leaf, bag of carrots, container of mushrooms, can of Rotel brand tomatoes and A-1 sauce, salt and pepper to taste and fill the remainder of the room with potatoes. Cover and cook on low heat for 6 to 8 hours. If the sour cream is used add to the pot one hour before serving.

SERVES: 8–10

Original recipe

Venison Crockpot Style

Submitted by Steve Ault
Richmond, Virginia

INGREDIENTS:

One large leg of venison, boned to fit
    your crock pot
Rotel brand tomatoes
Fresh mushrooms
Garlic salt or powder (your option)

Black pepper
Mrs. Dash (your favorite)
2 heads of broccoli or 1 head of
    cauliflower or a little of both
2 cans Rotel tomatoes

Place the venison in the crock-pot or Dutch oven, season with garlic powder or garlic salt to taste or, if not sure, use 2 teaspoons for starters. (Next time you can adjust), 1 tablespoon of Mrs. Dash seasonings, 2 tablespoons of black pepper or to taste. Add washed mushrooms (can is ok if fresh mushrooms are not available) dump 2 cans of Rotel tomatoes on top of ingredients and work tomatoes throughout the mixture. Cover and cook on low for 8 hours. Place broccoli and or cauliflower on top to steam until done just before you serve. Great over mashed potatoes, rice or pasta.

Grilled Leg of Venison

Submitted by Steve Ault
Richmond, Virginia

INGREDIENTS:

1 leg of venison front or hind quarter,
    bone in or bone out
1 large onion
1 large green pepper
Slice mushrooms, fresh or canned

4 strips of thick sliced bacon
Season salt
Italian dressing
Garlic buds or garlic powder

Cut the onion and green pepper into thick slices. Spread heavy aluminum foil out on counter long enough to cover both sides of the leg. Lay ½ of the onion, green pepper and mushrooms on the foil, sprinkle seasonings over items, lay 2 strips of bacon on veggies and lay the leg on all ingredients. Repeat the first step on top of the leg, pour ½ of the bottle of Italian dressing over the leg and fold the aluminum foil over the top of the leg. Wrap the entire leg at least three times to seal the leg tight. Place on the grill on low heat and turn every 15 minutes for 4 hours. Or place in the oven on 350° F for 3 hours or until the meat reaches 180°. Testing in the center of the meat. When cooking in the oven do not test meat until the last 15 to 20 minutes so you won't break the seal in the aluminum foil.

Grilled Venison Tenderloin

Submitted by Steve Ault
Richmond, Virginia

INGREDIENTS:

1 Venison Tenderloin
½ pound of thin sliced bacon

Season Salt

Cut tenderloin into 2 to 3 inch pieces. Wrap each piece with ½ slice of bacon, hold with a tooth pick. Sprinkle with season salt. Place on grill, watch the bacon because it will burn, put flame out with your favorite wine, beer or water. Cook to taste, medium is the best.

Venison Chili

Submitted by Steve Ault
Richmond, Virginia

INGREDIENTS:

8 pounds ground venison
4 pounds lean ground beef
3 pounds favorite bulk sausage
5 pounds onions, diced

15 packages chili seasoning mix (use
    different brands)
Various ingredients listed on seasoning
    packets

Ground chicken or turkey may be used in place of the ground beef. Extra meat may be added, along with other ingredients as needed.

In large pot, mix meat and onion. Cook until meat is brown; drain. Add all other ingredients and mix well. Cover and let simmer for 6 to 8 hours, stirring to keep the mixture from sticking to the bottom of the pan. Store in a cool place overnight. Reheat the next day, and simmer all day. Repeat another day if possible. Divide into containers and freeze until needed.

Note: This recipe was originally created for 15 pounds of meat. Amount can vary depending upon the quantity desired. Just be sure that venison is at least half the meat.

SERVES: Many

Pork Loin with Sausage Stuffing

Submitted by Carol Holt
Richmond, Virginia

MEAT INGREDIENTS:

3–4 pound pork loin
Chili powder

Steak seasoning (Adolph or Montrose)
5 tablespoons (or less) garlic powder

STUFFING INGREDIENTS:

1 cup chopped onion
6 ounces bulk Italian sausage
¼ cup raisins
½ cup parsley
⅓ cup soft bread crumbs

½ teaspoon fresh thyme or
    ½ teaspoon dried
½ teaspoon pepper
1 to 2 tablespoons water

SAUCE INGREDIENTS:

1 small jar peach or apricot preserves
1 jar fruit peach chutney

4 tablespoons white wine vinegar

Remove fat from loin. Rub meat with a mixture of up to 5 tablespoons of garlic powder and equal parts chili powder and steak seasoning. Wrap in foil and place in refrigerator over night.

Cook onion and sausage until meat is brown and onion is tender. Drain. Add raisins, parsley, bread crumbs, thyme and pepper. Drizzle with enough water to moisten, tossing lightly. Set aside.

Cut a pocket lengthwise through the thickest portion of the meat, cutting to within ½ inch of the other side. Fill pocket with stuffing and tie with twine. Cover with foil and bake at 350° F for 1½ hours or until meat thermometer registers 160–170° F. Remove from oven and brush on sauce.

Prepare sauce by combining preserves and chutney in saucepan. Bring to a boil. Add white wine vinegar. Simmer. If too thick, add a little water.

SERVES: 8 to 10

Cranberry Glazed Pork Roast

Submitted by Annette Gelber
Richmond, Virginia

INGREDIENTS:

4 pound boneless pork loin roast

2 cloves garlic-split

1½ tablespoons dried rosemary leaves

2 teaspoons cornstarch

¼ teaspoon cinnamon

⅛ teaspoon salt

½ teaspoon grated orange peel

2 tablespoons orange juice

2 tablespoons dry sherry

1 can (16 ounces) whole cranberry sauce

Rub roast with garlic cloves and dried rosemary leaves. Set aside.

In small saucepan, stir together the cornstarch, cinnamon, salt, orange peel, orange juice, sherry and cranberry sauce. Cook, stirring over medium heat until thickened. Set aside.

Place roast, uncovered, in shallow baking pan. Roast at 325° F for 30 to 35 minutes. Spoon ½ cup glaze over roast and continue roasting for 30 to 45 minutes more or until temperature is 155–160 degrees. Stand 10 minutes, then slice. Serve with remaining heated sauce.

SERVES: 14 to 16

Adapted from *Virginia's Finest*

Pork Chop Casserole

Submitted by Larry Jackson
Richmond, Virginia

INGREDIENTS:

6 pork chops (preferably without bone)
3 medium baking potatoes
2 cans cream of mushroom soup

1 can green beans or shelley beans, drained
1 cup grated cheddar cheese
Salt and pepper to taste

Prepare a 9 × 13″ baking dish by spraying it with Pam.

If necessary, remove bones from pork chops. Dredge in flour. Brown in vegetable oil in frying pan. Remove chops. To oil and bits remaining in pan, add salt and pepper, cream of mushroom soup and grated cheese. Heat until warm, cheese melts and mixture is blended.

Peel and thinly slice potatoes. Place in layers in prepared pan. Top with beans. Place chops on top of beans. Pour sauce mixture over chops. Cover with foil and bake at 350° F for 1½ hours or more. Uncover for last 10 to 15 minutes to slightly brown.

Chicken breasts or turkey medallions may be substituted for the pork chops.

SERVES: 3

Family recipe

Party Ham and Chicken

Submitted by Nell Gregory
Richmond, Virginia

INGREDIENTS:

8 chicken breasts halves, boned and
    skinned
8 slices bacon

½ slice Smithfield ham per breast
1 can cream of mushroom soup
½ pint sour cream

Grease casserole. Place ham on bottom. Wrap bacon around chicken breast. Place on ham. Mix soup and sour cream. Pour over chicken. Refrigerate or bake 3 hours at 275° F uncovered.

Note: May be prepared ahead and cooked later.

SERVES: 8

Family recipe

Pulled Turkey Barbecue

Submitted by Jane Whitaker
Richmond, Virginia

INGREDIENTS:

2 large onions, chopped
1 large garlic clove, minced
2 cups cider vinegar
½ stick unsalted butter
½ cup ketchup

3 tablespoons Worcestershire
2 tablespoons Tabasco
1 tablespoon salt
1 tablespoon fresh ground pepper
4½–5 pound turkey breast

Mix onion, garlic, vinegar, butter, ketchup, worcestershire, Tobasco, salt and pepper in a 6 quart heavy saucepan. Simmer 15 minutes, then add 4½ to 5 pound turkey breast, skin discarded, cavity side down. Cook at a bare simmer, covered, 2½ hours. Reserving sauce in pan, transfer turkey to a cutting board. Let cool then shred turkey meat and stir into remaining sauce. Simmer over low heat for 1½ hours more, stirring occasionally. Check for additional seasonings.

YIELDS: 8 cups

Old recipe—source unknown

Poppy Seed Chicken

Submitted by Wendy Cole
Sanford, North Carolina

INGREDIENTS:

3 cups cooked deboned chicken
1 can cream of mushroom soup
1 cup chicken broth
1 cup (8 ounces) sour cream

1 tablespoon poppy seeds
1 stick margarine
1 sleeve crushed Ritz crackers

Mix chicken, mushroom soup, chicken broth, and sour cream. Spray a 9 × 13 pan and pour mixture in. Melt the margarine. Add crackers and poppy seeds to margarine. Mix well and sprinkle over chicken mixture. Bake at 350° F until it bubbles.

SERVES: 6

Family recipe

Hot Chicken Salad

Submitted by Georgia C. Daniels
Chester, Virginia

INGREDIENTS:

Boneless chicken breasts - 4 halves
1 cup celery, chopped
1 cup mayonnaise — Kraft regular
1 can (10½ ounces) mushroom soup —
    Campbells regular

1½ teaspoons fresh lemon juice
1 cup shredded cheese — Kraft sharp
    cheddar
2 teaspoons chopped green onions
White bread (2 to 4 slices) buttered

Cook chicken breasts very gently in salted water so they will be done but not tough. Cut chicken into pieces. Add to mushroom soup and mayonnaise. Add lemon juice and grated sharp cheese and chopped onion. Mix well. Toast bread lightly so it is light in color and hot. Spread with butter. Cut into one inch square pieces. Put chicken mixture in heat-proof dish. Put bread on top. Bake at 350° F for 30 minutes.

Note: This may be made ahead. Refrigerate if not baking immediately.

SERVES: 4

Friend — Joan Greason

Chicken Hash

Submitted by Annette Gelber
Richmond, Virginia

INGREDIENTS:

4 tablespoons butter
4 tablespoons flour
1 teaspoon salt
½ teaspoon white pepper
4 cups milk
1 cup half-and-half
½ teaspoon Worcestershire sauce

8 drops hot pepper sauce
½ cup Sherry
4 cups diced, cooked chicken (white
  meat only)
4 egg yolks, beaten
Cooked wild rice—enough for 4 servings

Cook wild rice separately according to package directions. You will need ¾ of a cup of hot COOKED rice for each serving—or more if desired.

Melt butter in medium saucepan. Blend in flour, salt and pepper. Stir in milk and half-and-half. Heat to boiling (stirring constantly). Boil 1 minute. Stir in Worcestershire sauce, 6 drops of hot pepper sauce and Sherry. Stir in chicken; season to taste. Add 2 drops of hot sauce to egg yolks. Return all to saucepan. Pour into shallow, lightly greased, heat proof serving dish. Put the dish under the broiler until contents are browned and bubbly. Place each serving on a bed of hot wild rice.

Suggestion: Serve with a spinach salad.

SERVES: 4

Crickets Restaurant—Chicago

Sweet Sour Chicken

Submitted by Pat Glupker
Richmond, Virginia

INGREDIENTS:

2 tablespoons cornstarch
¼ cup sugar
¼ cup vinegar
1 cup pineapple juice
½ teaspoon garlic salt
1 tablespoon soy sauce
1 pound boneless, skinless chicken
    breasts, cut in 1″ pieces

2 tablespoons cooking oil
1 each medium green pepper and red
    pepper, cut in 1″ pieces
1 medium onion, sliced into rings
1 cup sliced mushrooms
Sliced almonds or crisp Chinese noodles

Combine cornstarch, sugar, vinegar, pineapple juice, garlic salt and soy sauce in saucepan and heat, stirring constantly, until thickened. Saute chicken quickly in hot oil until no longer pink. Add chicken to sauce. Cover and keep warm. Just before serving stir in peppers, onion and mushrooms. Cover and cook for 3 minutes or until vegetables are softened. Stir and serve over rice. Top with sliced almonds or Chinese (crisp) noodles.

SERVES: 4

Original recipe

Chicken Tetrazzini

Submitted by Candy Cecil
Midlothian, Virginia

INGREDIENTS:

1 can cream of mushroom soup, undiluted
2 cans cream of chicken soup, undiluted
3 cups chopped cooked chicken breast
12 ounces fat-free sour cream

1 pound spaghetti noodles
1 cup shredded Parmesan cheese
Paprika
¾ stick margarine (melted)

Cook noodles and drain. Mix noodles, soups, sour cream, margarine and chicken together and pour in 9×12×2½″ pan sprayed with Pam. Top with Parmesan cheese and paprika.

Bake at 350° F for 30 minutes or until bubbling.

SERVES: 10 to 12

Source unknown

Chicken Parmigiana

Submitted by Billie L. Cummings
Burke, Virginia

INGREDIENTS:

2 cans tomato sauce
¼ teaspoon basil
3 or 4 drops Worcestershire sauce
1 clove of garlic, minced
1 tablespoon butter/margarine
2 eggs, beaten
1 teaspoon salt

Freshly ground pepper to taste
2 pounds skinned, boned chicken breasts
¾ cup bread crumbs
Olive oil
Parmesan cheese
½ pound mozzarella cheese, sliced

Combine tomato sauce, basil, Worcestershire, garlic and butter in a saucepan. Bring to a boil; simmer 10 minutes. Mix eggs, salt, and pepper. Dip chicken in egg mix, then in bread crumbs. Pour olive oil into skillet to cover bottom; heat. Brown chicken; drain. Arrange, slightly overlapping, in a 8 × 12 casserole dish; cover with tomato sauce. Sprinkle generously with Parmesan cheese; cover tightly. Bake 350° F for 45 minutes to an hour. Arrange mozzarella cheese over meat. Bake about 10 minutes longer.

Note: The original recipe called for veal instead of chicken.

SERVES: 4 to 6

The Garden Club Cookbook (1969)

Chicken Orange and Barbeque

Submitted by Babs Jackson,
President/CEO, HHH

INGREDIENTS:

3 large fryers   Lawry's Seasoning

SAUCE INGREDIENTS:

1 can frozen orange juice   ¾ cup BBQ sauce
¾ cup sugar

Cut up 3 large fryers, season with Lawry's and place in large foil-lined baking pan.

Mix together in saucepan: 1 can undiluted frozen orange juice, sugar and barbeque sauce. Heat until sugar dissolves. Pour over chicken. Bake at 325°–350° F, covered, for about 1 hour. Turn up heat and uncover at end to brown. Baste frequently.

SERVES: 10 to 12

Family recipe

Chicken and Broccoli Casserole

Submitted by Candy Cecil
Midlothian, Virginia

INGREDIENTS:

4 cups cooked diced chicken breasts   1 cup mayonnaise
1 16-ounce bag frozen broccoli florets   1 cup shredded cheddar cheese
2 cans cream of mushroom soup   1 12-ounce bag stuffing mix
2 cans cream of celery soup

Cook and dice chicken. Cook and drain broccoli. Spray bottom and sides of 9×12×2½″ pan with Pam. Line bottom with broccoli, then chicken. Combine soups, mayonnaise, and cheese and spread over chicken. Top with stuffing mix and bake at 350° F for 30 minutes or until heated through.

SERVES: 10 to 12

Source unknown

Curried Chicken

Submitted by Kate Yoffy
Richmond, Virginia

INGREDIENTS:

¼ cup flour
1½ teaspoons curry powder
1½ teaspoons onion powder
½ teaspoon turmeric
¼ teaspoon ginger
¼ teaspoon dry mustard

Ground red pepper to taste
3 pounds chicken pieces, skinned
¼ cup vegetable oil
½ cup dry white wine
½ cup water

Combine flour, curry powder, onion powder, turmeric, ginger, dry mustard, and red pepper. Dredge the chicken pieces in the flour mixture. Reserve any leftover flour mixture.

Heat the vegetable oil in a skillet. Cook chicken over medium heat turning once. Remove chicken.

Add reserved flour to the frying pan and cook one minute stirring constantly. Add wine and water. Cook, stirring, over medium heat, until mixture has thickened.

Add chicken, cover, and cook 30 minutes or until chicken is cooked throughout.

SERVES: 4

Source unknown

Chicken Casserole

Submitted by Hannah Gallier
Richmond, Virginia

INGREDIENTS:

6 chicken breasts
Salt, pepper, paprika
1 stick butter or margarine
¼ teaspoon basil
¼ teaspoon rosemary
½ cup chopped onions

1 small can mushrooms
½ cup slivered almonds
¼ cup cooking sherry
1 can cream of mushroom soup
Rice cooked separately

Place chicken in baking dish. Sprinkle with salt, pepper, and paprika. In another skillet, melt butter or margarine. Add all other ingredients except rice and pour over chicken. Cook 1 hour and 15 minutes in 350° F oven. Cook rice separately. Place cooked rice on large meat platter, place chicken on top and cover with mushroom gravy and let guests or family serve themselves.

SERVES: 6

Source unknown

Aunt Gladys' Chicken Baked with Broccoli

Submitted by Kate Yoffy
Richmond, Virginia

INGREDIENTS:

5 whole chicken breasts, halved and
    remove skin
2 bunches raw broccoli, cut into spears
2 cans artichoke hearts
2 cans cream of chicken soup

¾ cup mayonnaise
1 teaspoon curry powder (or more to taste)
1½ cups grated, sharp cheddar cheese
Buttered bread crumbs

In an oven-to-table baking dish, layer the raw broccoli. Scatter the artichoke hearts over the broccoli. Place the chicken breasts, in a single layer, on top of broccoli and artichoke hearts.

In a small bowl, combine soup, mayonnaise, and curry powder. Spoon mixture on top of chicken. Top with grated cheddar cheese and bread crumbs.

Bake, uncovered, in a 350° F oven for 1½ hours until chicken is done.

Note: This is a marvelous "do ahead" company dish. It can be put together the day before. Just cover tightly and refrigerate. Remember to bring it to room temperature before baking. (If chicken is very cold, baking time might have to be increased.)

SERVES: 8 to 10

Family recipe

Chicken Provencal

Submitted by Suzanne Lunsford
Richmond, Virginia

INGREDIENTS:

4 tablespoons olive oil
1 large onion, chopped
3 large garlic cloves, chopped
1 28-ounce can diced peeled tomatoes, undrained
3 3 × ½″ strips orange peel (orange part only)

2½ teaspoons oregano
2 bay leaves
½ teaspoon paprika
4 boneless, skinless chicken breasts

Heat 2 tablespoons oil in heavy large saucepan. Add onion and garlic and sauté over medium heat until tender, about 10 minutes. Add undrained tomatoes, orange peel, oregano, bay leaves and paprika and cook until sauce thickens, stirring occasionally, about 30 minutes. Discard bay leaves.

Heat remaining 2 tablespoons oil in another heavy skillet over medium high heat. Season chicken with salt and pepper. Add chicken to skillet and sauté until cooked through, about 5 minutes per side. Transfer to plate. Rewarm sauce and spoon over chicken.

SERVES: 4–8

Source unknown

Chicken Prunella

Submitted by Fran Gregory
Richmond, Virginia

(A Variation of Chicken Marbella)

INGREDIENTS:

4 pounds fresh, skinless, boneless chicken breasts, cut in half or quartered
1½–2 cups pitted dried prunes, quartered
½ cup olive oil
½ to ¾ cup whole, pitted or stuffed Spanish green olives
½ cup capers, with or without juice
1 to 1½ large heads fresh garlic, peeled and chopped

½ cup red wine vinegar
½ cup dried oregano
6 to 8 bay leaves, whole
Salt and pepper to taste
1 cup white wine
¼ cup fresh chopped cilantro
Brown sugar (optional)

Mix chicken, prunes, oil, olives, capers, garlic, red wine, oregano, bay leaves, salt and pepper well in a large bowl. Cover and marinate overnight in the refrigerator.

When ready to cook, preheat oven to 350° F.

Place chicken in one layer in baking dish(es) and cover with marinade. Sprinkle with brown sugar if desired. Pour the white wine gently around and between pieces of chicken. Bake for 30 minutes, then check the chicken for doneness by sticking with a fork. The juice should be yellow rather than pink. Cook an additional 15 minutes or more if necessary.

Put the chicken on a serving platter, and with a slotted spoon, cover it with the prunes, capers and olives. Drizzle some of the remaining juice over this, and sprinkle with the chopped cilantro. The remaining juice can be placed on the table for those who like more, but chicken will be very moist and tender without it. Serve with basmati rice.

Note: Although this recipe is not as simple as one might like, it is certainly worth the extra time and effort to prepare. It is delicious, can be served hot or at room temperature, serves 10 to 12, and makes wonderful leftovers. Adjust ingredients to personal taste.

SERVES: 10 to 12

Salmon with Fresh Herbs over Mashed Potatoes with Tomato Sauce

Submitted by Jane Whitaker
Richmond, Virginia

INGREDIENTS:

Salmon	Olive oil
Fresh bread crumbs	Salt and pepper
Fresh basil and other herbs (your choice)	Potatoes, mashed
Bottled horseradish	Marinara or tomato sauce

In processor combine fresh bread crumbs, any fresh herbs you like and bottled horseradish, salt and pepper.

Salt and pepper individual portions of salmon. Brush with olive oil. Press bread crumbs mixture onto salmon and drizzle with olive oil. Bake 425° F for 10 minutes.

In processor make basil oil by pureeing fresh basil and slowly adding olive oil, salt and pepper. Mash potatoes and add some of the basil oil at the last minute.

Bring any good quality marinara or tomato sauce to simmer.

To serve: Spoon potatoes onto center of plate. Top with salmon. Spoon tomato sauce around potatoes. Drizzle sauce with a little more basil oil.

SERVES: (depends on amount of salmon)

Source unknown

Salmon Bake with Pecan Crunch Crust

Submitted by Ann Bendheim
Richmond, Virginia

INGREDIENTS:

2 tablespoons Dijon mustard
2 tablespoons butter, melted
1 tablespoon PLUS 1 teaspoon honey
¼ cup EACH: bread crumbs, finely
    chopped pecans OR walnuts

2 teaspoons chopped fresh parsley
4 6-ounce salmon filets
Salt and pepper to taste

Preheat oven to 450° F. Mix mustard, butter and honey in a bowl and set aside. In another bowl, mix bread crumbs, pecans and parsley. Season salmon with salt and pepper to taste and place on ungreased baking sheet or broiler pan. Brush each fillet with mustard-honey mixture and top with a spoonful of crumb coating. Bake 10 minutes per inch of thickness or until salmon flakes when tested with a fork.

SERVES: 4

Source unknown

Stuffed Baby Coho Salmon

Submitted by Larry Jackson
Richmond, Virginia

INGREDIENTS:

4 8-ounce Coho salmon (or trout)
10 ounce package frozen chopped spinach,
    cooked and drained thoroughly
3 tablespoons butter
¼ pound fresh mushrooms, chopped

1 small onion, chopped
¼ cup parsley, chopped
2 cloves garlic, minced or pressed
½ teaspoon dill weed
½ teaspoon beau monde

Melt butter in medium sized skillet, add onion and mushrooms, saute 5 minutes over medium heat. Add garlic, cook 2 minutes longer. Stir in spinach, parsley, dill and beau monde. Mix well. Remove from heat and cool until able to handle.

Stuff each salmon with spinach mixture. Do not overstuff. Place stuffed fish in grilling basket. Brush with melted butter. Cook over charcoal fire, brushing periodically with melted butter, until salmon flakes (approximately 20 minutes, depending upon heat of fire).

SERVES: 4

Original recipe

Spicy Grilled Salmon Steaks with Black Butter

Submitted by Kathie Markel
Richmond, Virginia

INGREDIENTS:

1½ teaspoon freshly ground black pepper
½ teaspoon paprika
¼ teaspoon cayenne
1 teaspoon minced garlic
1 tablespoon minced onion
½ teaspoon crumbled dried thyme

¼ teaspoon salt
1 tablespoon olive oil
2 salmon steaks (1 pound) each, about
   1 inch thick
1 tablespoon unsalted butter

In a bowl stir together black pepper, paprika, cayenne, garlic, onion, thyme, salt, and oil until the mixture forms a stiff paste. Pat the paste onto both sides of each salmon steak. Heat an oiled, ridged grill pan over moderately high heat until it is smoking and in it sauté the salmon for 3 to 4 minutes on each side, or until it is cooked through. While the salmon is cooking, in a small skillet cook the butter over moderate heat (swirling the skillet) until butter is dark brown, but do not let it burn. Transfer the salmon to heated plates and pour the butter over it.

SERVES: 2

Adapted from epicurious.com

Broiled Salmon with Basting Sauce

Submitted by Ann Yoffy
Richmond, Virginia

INGREDIENTS:

6 tablespoons grade B maple syrup
½ cup water
2 tablespoons minced peeled fresh
   ginger root

2 garlic cloves minced
1 teaspoon dried hot pepper flakes
½ teaspoon salt
4 1″ thick salmon filets

In a small heavy saucepan combine first 6 ingredients and simmer until reduced to about ½ cup. Cool basting sauce. Arrange salmon on broiler and season with salt. Broil 4 minutes. Brush salmon with sauce and broil until just cooked through, about 6 minutes.

SERVES: 4

Adapted from *Gourmet* Magazine

Baked Virginia Rockfish

Submitted by Ed Tillet
Midlothian, Virginia

INGREDIENTS:

1 4–6-pound striped bass, freshly caught
  or purchased
1 medium purple or white onion
¼ stick butter

6 slices of bacon
2 ribs of celery
2 tablespoons Old Bay Seasoning
⅛ cup olive or vegetable oil

Clean and scale the fish. Rockfish, or striped bass, are best when caught in late fall. (Cook with head-on for nice presentation!)

Cut the fish to the bone twice on both sides at equal distance back from where the head was removed (as if attempting to cut into steaks). Place slices of onion and a pat of butter in each incision. Sprinkle liberally with Old Bay. Place the two ribs of celery, including leaves, into length of fish abdominal cavity. Add some onion pieces to cavity. Wrap three pieces of bacon around fish at a 45 degree angle and complete with other three pieces going the opposite direction to form a lacing effect. Place on shallow pan covered in aluminum foil and oiled liberally with vegetable or olive oil to prevent sticking.

Place in cold oven and set temperature to 325° F. When bacon is crisp and completely done, so is the fish. Remove and let cool for approximately 10 minutes before serving to allow meat to firm up. Lift off carefully and serve on long platter. Garnish with sliced lemon and parsley. (Score the skin along the dorsal fin and lift steaks off of fish carcass, serving skin side down. Crumble bacon pieces over individual servings.)

SERVES: 4 to 6 (depending on size of fish)

Original recipe

Horseradish Crusted Rockfish

Submitted by Annette Gelber
Richmond, Virginia

INGREDIENTS:

4 rockfish fillets (6 ounces each)
2 tablespoons horseradish
½ teaspoon minced garlic
1 pinch white pepper

⅓ cup mayonnaise
1 tablespoon bread crumbs
1 anchovy fillet (optional)
Flour to coat

Blend horseradish, garlic, white pepper, mayonnaise, bread crumbs and anchovy fillet in food processor. Dredge rockfish in flour; coat with horseradish mixture. Moderately grease baking pan with oil. Place fish in pan in one layer and pre-heat oven to 350° F. Bake 9 to 12 minutes until fish flakes easily with a fork.

SERVES: 4

Source unknown

Grilled Grouper with Sun-Dried Tomato Butter

Submitted by Lesley Greenberg
Richmond, Virginia

INGREDIENTS:

1½ pound grouper filets
4 ounces butter
¼ cup sun-dried tomatoes

½ teaspoon garlic, minced
2 teaspoons basil, fresh, chopped

Allow the butter to reach room temperature. Soak the tomatoes in warm water until soft. Drain and add to food processor. Pulse until pureed. Add garlic, basil, and butter and pulse until just mixed. Place on wax paper or parchment and roll into a cylinder. Refrigerate. Grill fish. Thinly (¼ inch) slice the prepared (cold) butter. Place two slices on top of hot fish. Serve immediately.

SERVES: 4

Source unknown

Suzy's Shrimp Casserole

Submitted by Marsha Ginther
Midlothian, Virginia

INGREDIENTS:

1 box Uncle Ben's wild long grain rice
1 can mushrooms, stems and pieces
4 cloves garlic, minced
½ stick margarine

1 8-ounce package frozen cooked shrimp,
    thawed
or 1 12-ounce package frozen lagostina
or 20 ounces shrimp, cooked

Cook rice according to directions. Melt margarine, add drained mushrooms, garlic and seafood. Mix with cooked rice and place into casserole. Cover and bake at 350° F for 45 minutes.
Note: Remember to defrost shrimp the night before.

SERVES: 4

Family recipe

Shrimp in Wild Rice

Submitted by Becky McCann
Richmond, Virginia

INGREDIENTS:

½ cup flour
1 cup melted butter or margarine divided
4 cups chicken broth
¼ teaspoon white pepper
1 cup thinly sliced onions
½ cup thinly sliced green peppers

1 cup thinly sliced mushroom
2 pounds cooked, peeled, deveined shrimp
2 tablespoons Worcestershire sauce
Few drops hot sauce
4 cups cooked wild rice—set aside

Gradually add flour to ½ cup melted butter and stir constantly over low heat until bubbly. Gradually add broth and stir until smooth and thickened. Add white pepper and simmer 2 to 3 minutes. Sauté onion, green peppers and mushrooms in remaining ½ cup butter. Drain. Combine white sauce, sautéed vegetables and 2 pounds shrimp, 2 tablespoons Worcestershire sauce and few drops of hot sauce. Spoon into casserole and bake at 300° F for 45 to 50 minutes. Serve over hot cooked rice.

SERVES: 4–6

Source unknown

Shrimp Sauté Vin Blanc

Submitted by Annette Gelber
Richmond, Virginia

INGREDIENTS:

1 pound large raw shrimp, shelled and
deveined, (approximately 4 to 5
per person)
2 tablespoons sweet butter

1 tablespoon chopped shallots
¾ cup dry white wine
¾ cup whipping cream
Minced parsley for garnish

Cook shrimp in butter in skillet or chafing dish 2 minutes. Add shallots; cook 1½ minutes. Deglaze pan with wine. Remove shrimp from utensil and keep warm. Boil wine rapidly on high, in same pan, to reduce volume by half. Add cream. Cook 3 minutes; pour over shrimp. Garnish with parsley.

SERVES: 4

Cricket's Bistro — Chicago

Shrimp Creole

Submitted by Paulette Wagner
Prince George, Virginia

INGREDIENTS:

2 tablespoons oil
2 tablespoons flour
1 cup chopped green onion
¼ teaspoon garlic juice
½ cup chopped green pepper
1 can (14½ ounce) stewed tomatoes

1 teaspoon pepper
1 teaspoon salt
¼ cup parsley
2 cups shrimp, cleaned and deveined
1 can cream of mushroom soup
Rice

Heat oil, add flour and stir until golden brown. Add onions, garlic, green peppers, tomatoes, salt and pepper. Cook until onions are tender. Add shrimp, parsley, and soup, cook about 6 minutes. Remove from heat.

Let creole sit while you make the rice. Serve over rice.

SERVES: 4 to 6

Family recipe

Shrimp 'N' Grits

Submitted by Emily Morley
Midlothian, Virginia

INGREDIENTS:

1 cup quick cooking grits
Salt to taste
White pepper to taste
Cayenne pepper to taste
Nutmeg to taste
1 cup shredded cheddar cheese
6 slices bacon

2 tablespoons oil
1 pound raw shrimp
1 pint fresh mushrooms, sliced
1 cup green onions, sliced
1 clove garlic, minced
1 teaspoon hot pepper sauce
1 tablespoon fresh parsley, chopped

Cook grits according to directions on package. Add seasonings and cheese, set aside. Keep warm. Fry 6 slices bacon until crisp, drain, set aside.

Cook shrimp in 2 tablespoons oil until pink. Add mushrooms and saute 2 minutes. Add green onions, crumbled bacon, garlic, hot pepper sauce, parsley. Divide grits into 4 servings and spoon shrimp mixture on top.

SERVES: 4

Phoebe Olson

Seafood Pie

Submitted by Pat Glupker
Richmond, Virginia

INGREDIENTS:

1 6½-ounce can albacore tuna
1 onion, coarsely chopped
2 hard-cooked eggs, sliced
1 can mushroom soup

1 teaspoon Worcestershire
Pepper to taste
3 cups mashed potatoes
⅓ cup grated cheese

Combine tuna, onion and egg in a shallow baking dish. Blend soup, Worcestershire sauce and pepper and spread over tuna mixture. Spread the mashed potatoes around the edges and sprinkle potatoes with cheese. Bake at 350° F for 30 minutes. *Note:* Can substitute shrimp, crab or combination for the tuna.

SERVES: 4

Hawaiian Electric Company

Seafood Casserole

Submitted by Gloria Keeton
Midlothian, Virginia

INGREDIENTS:

16 ounces cream cheese
1 can cream of shrimp soup
Milk to make sauce soupy
6–8 ounces noodles (use any kind you
    prefer: bowtie, spaghetti, linguini)

1 pound of seafood (use any combination
    you prefer: crab, lobster, scallops)
¼ pound butter

Combine cheese, soup and milk (for sauce) in double boiler. Cook noodles and drain. Combine and place in casserole. Bake at 350° F until bubbly. This can be frozen and then cooked. Clam chowder may be substituted for shrimp soup. Seafood may be varied.

SERVES: 4

Source unknown

Baked Seafood Casserole

Submitted by Esther M. Grandstaff
Richmond, Virginia

INGREDIENTS:

1 pound lump crabmeat
½ pound large cooked shrimp
1 cup mayonnaise
½ cup chopped green peppers

½ cup chopped mushrooms (canned)
½ cup chopped celery
1 tablespoon Worcestershire sauce
2 cups coarsely crushed potato chips

Combine together crabmeat, shrimp, mayonnaise, green peppers, mushrooms, celery and Worcestershire sauce.

Place the combined ingredients in a greased 2½ quart casserole.

Sprinkle potato chips on top and sprinkle with paprika.

Bake at 400° F for 25 minutes.

SERVES: 6

Original recipe

Crab in Shells

Submitted by Mary Morgan
Midlothian, Virginia

INGREDIENTS:

1 pound lump or backfin crabmeat
2 tablespoons dry sherry
⅔ cup mayonnaise
Lemon juice to taste

Salt and pepper to taste
Buttered bread crumbs
4–5 Seafood shells

Mix crabmeat, sherry, mayonnaise, lemon juice and salt and pepper together. Divide into 4 or 5 seafood shells. Top with buttered bread crumbs. Bake at 350° F for 15 or 20 minutes or until bubbly.

SERVES: 4 or 5

Original recipe

Deluxe Crabmeat

Submitted by Barbara Anchell
Richmond, Virginia

INGREDIENTS:

1 pound jumbo lump crab meat
1 large egg
1 tablespoon dry or golden sherry
2 tablespoons regular mayonnaise

Salt and pepper
Bread crumbs tossed with melted butter
  (optional)
Seafood shells (or ramekins)

Pick through crab for shells, but try not to break up lumps. Mix together the egg, sherry, mayonnaise, salt and pepper and then fold in the crab. Put mixture into buttered (or sprayed with vegetable spray) individual shells or ramekins or one 9″ pie plate. Top with buttered bread crumbs, if desired. Bake at 350° F for 15 to 20 minutes, uncovered.

SERVES: 4

Family recipe

Pasta
and
Rice

Pineapple-Noodle Casserole

Submitted by Babs Jackson,
President/CEO

INGREDIENTS:

1 package (8–10 ounces) egg noodles
¼ cup butter
⅔ cup heated milk
3 eggs, well beaten
1 teaspoon salt

Dash cinnamon
Squeeze of lemon
1 can (20 ounces) crushed pineapple,
    drained
Crushed corn flakes

Cook noodles according to package directions. Drain well. Mix butter, milk and eggs together. Add salt, cinnamon, lemon, pineapple and noodles. Place in greased 9″×13″ casserole. Top with crushed corn flakes. Bake in 350° F oven for 30 minutes.

SERVES: 6 to 8

5000 Years in the Kitchen — Temple Emanu-el, Dallas, TX

Noodle Pudding

Submitted by Jean Goldman
Richmond, Virginia

PUDDING INGREDIENTS:

6 large eggs, separated
½ pound (8 ounces) medium noodles,
     cooked
1 pound creamed cottage cheese
½ pound (8 ounces) cream cheese (brick)

4 heaping tablespoons sour cream
¾ stick butter, melted
½ cup sugar
Pinch of salt

Beat egg whites until stiff. Set aside. Beat 6 yolks. Set aside. Boil noodles. Drain. Mix egg yolks, creamed cottage cheese, cream cheese, sour cream, melted butter, sugar and salt with electric mixer (at medium speed) until well blended. Add noodles. Mix by hand until blended. Fold in egg whites. Pour into greased $13 \times 9 \times 2''$ dish.

TOPPING INGREDIENTS:

¼ pound butter
½ cup sugar

⅔ cup plus 2 tablespoons graham cracker
     crumbs

Melt butter. Add sugar and crumbs. Sprinkle over noodles. Bake at 350° F for 1 hour. Serve warm, room temperature or cold.

Note: May be made with light or fat free cottage cheese, cream cheese, and sour cream.

SERVES: 12 to 16

Friend's recipe

Spinach Lasagna

Submitted by Margie Gunn
Richmond, Virginia

INGREDIENTS:

Reynolds Wrap® Release™ Non-Stick Foil
1 container (15 ounces) ricotta cheese
2 packages (10 ounce *each*) frozen chopped
  spinach, thawed, squeezed dry
1½ cups grated Parmesan cheese, divided

3 eggs
2 jars (28 ounces *each*) pasta sauce
12 lasagna noodles, cooked and drained
1 package (16 ounces) shredded
  Mozzarella cheese

Preheat oven to 350° F. Line a 13×9×2-inch baking pan with Reynolds Wrap Release Non-Stick Foil with non-stick side toward food; set aside.

Combine ricotta cheese, spinach, 1 cup Parmesan cheese and eggs in a large bowl; set aside. Spread 1½ cups pasta sauce in Release foil-lined pan. Arrange 3 noodles over sauce in a single layer; spoon 1½ cups ricotta mixture over noodles. Sprinkle with 1 cup Mozzarella cheese.

Repeat layering process two times. Arrange last 3 noodles over Mozzarella cheese; spoon remaining sauce, Mozzarella and Parmesan cheeses on top.

Cover with non-stick foil with non-stick side toward food. Bake 45 minutes. Remove foil cover and continue baking 15 minutes or until cheese is melted. Let stand 15 minutes before serving.

Reynolds Kitchens Tip: For easy cleanup, use 2 sheets of Reynolds Wrap Release Non-Stick Foil to make one large sheet that will completely line a large baking pan. Here's how: Stack 2 foil sheets with non-stick sides together. Fold edges on one long side over twice. Open foil; press seam flat. Flip pan upside down. Place foil sheet with non-stick side toward pan. Press foil around pan. Remove foil. Flip pan upright; drop foil inside. Non-stick side should be toward your food. Crimp foil edges to rim of pan.

Note: This is a recipe from the Reynolds Kitchens of the Reynolds Consumer Division. I am employed there and the "Kitchens" are proud to submit this recipe for your book.

SERVES: 6 to 8

Reynolds Kitchens recipe

Baked Spaghetti

Submitted by Candy Cecil
Midlothian, Virginia

INGREDIENTS:

1 pound spaghetti
1 quart Ragú sauce
1 cup cheddar cheese, grated
2 cups shredded mozzarella cheese

Seasonings: oregano, basil, Italian
    seasoning, red pepper flakes
Pam cooking spray
1 cup shredded Parmesan cheese

Cook spaghetti and drain. Put in greased $9 \times 12 \times 2\frac{1}{2}''$ pan. Add 1 quart sauce, 1 cup cheddar cheese, 2 cups mozzarella. Sprinkle with 1 teaspoon each of desired spices, stir to mix.

TOPPING INGREDIENTS:

1 cup Parmesan cheese, shredded
¾ teaspoon each: oregano, basil, Italian
    seasoning, red pepper flakes

2 tablespoons fresh parsley, chopped

Top with 1 cup Parmesan cheese, basil, Italian seasoning, oregano, red pepper flakes and parsley.

Bake at 350° F until bubbly, approximately 30 to 35 minutes.

SERVES: 10 to 12

Source unknown

Lasagna

Submitted by Babs Jackson,
President/CEO, HHH

INGREDIENTS:

8 ounces lasagna noodles (12)
1 tablespoon olive oil
1 pound ground round
½ clove garlic, minced (or more to taste)
1 tablespoon dried parsley flakes
½ teaspoon salt
½ teaspoon dried oregano leaves
½ teaspoon dried sweet basil leaves
½ teaspoon sugar
1 6-ounce can tomato paste
1 15-ounce can tomato sauce

¼ cup water
1 16-ounce container cottage cheese (or
    8-ounce cottage cheese and 8-ounce
    ricotta cheese)
1 egg, slightly beaten
1 tablespoon dried parsley flakes
½ teaspoon salt
⅛ teaspoon pepper
1 pound mozzarella cheese slices
½ cup grated Parmesan cheese

Cook noodles according to package directions, rinse and hold in cold water to prevent sticking. Drain thoroughly before using.

Brown meat in oil. Drain. Add garlic, parsley, salt, oregano, basil, sugar, tomato paste, tomato sauce, and water. Bring to boil, reduce heat to low, simmer uncovered for 15 minutes.

In small bowl, combine cottage cheese, egg, parsley, salt, pepper, and ¼ pound of mozzarella, finely diced.

Pour enough meat sauce in 2 quart dish to barely cover the bottom. Add ⅓ noodles, ⅓ cottage cheese mix, ⅓ Parmesan cheese, ⅓ mozzarella slices, ⅓ remaining meat sauce. Repeat layers, ending with meat sauce. Cover with light weight aluminum foil. Bake at 375° F for 25 minutes. Remove cover and bake 5 minutes longer. Let stand for 5 minutes before cutting into squares to serve.

SERVES: 8 to 10

Source unknown

Thick and Spicy Spaghetti Sauce

Submitted by Jane H. Settle-Stanley
Arlington, Virginia

INGREDIENTS:

2 pounds 'hot' Italian sausage
1 large onion, chopped
1 large (or 2 small) can(s) of mushrooms,
    bits and pieces with most of liquid
¼ cup fresh basil, chopped

2 tablespoons minced garlic
2 8-ounce cans tomato sauce
1 tablespoon sugar
1 teaspoon salt (or more to taste)

Remove sausage from links and brown in large skillet in two batches. Drain and transfer to 5 quart Dutch oven (or saucepan). Combine chopped onion, mushrooms with most of liquid, basil, and garlic into skillet and sauté. Combine with sausage. Add tomato sauce. Bring to boil. Stir and turn heat to simmer. Add salt and sugar. Let simmer for at least 1 hour. Serve over your favorite pasta and freeze the rest in portions appropriate for your family.

Note: Seasonings are approximate and may be adjusted according to taste.

SERVES: 8 to 10

Original recipe

Pesto Sauce for Pasta

Submitted by Sallie Grant
Richmond, Virginia

INGREDIENTS:

2 cups fresh basil
1 garlic clove
¼ cup pine nuts

¼ cup Parmesan cheese
½ cup olive oil, divided
Salt to taste

Chop basil, garlic and nuts very finely in a blender with 2 tablespoons of the olive oil. Mix in Parmesan cheese slowly. Then add the rest of the olive oil in small amounts. Salt to taste and mix again. Can be refrigerated or frozen for later use.

Note: Can also be used on tomato salad.

SERVES: 4

Family recipe

Macaroni and Cheese Casserole

Submitted by Geneva Frizzell
Blacksburg, Virginia

INGREDIENTS:

1 (8 ounce) package elbow macaroni
12 ounces cheddar cheese, shredded
1 cup Swiss cheese, shredded
2¼ cups milk

3 large eggs, lightly beaten
1½ teaspoon salt
¼ teaspoon ground white pepper

Cook macaroni according to package directions (about 6 to 7 minutes), drain. Layer macaroni with the Swiss and cheddar cheese in a lightly greased 2 quart casserole. Combine milk, eggs, salt and pepper. Pour over macaroni and cheese. Cover. Bake 350° F for 45 minutes. Uncover, sprinkle with paprika. Cover and let stand 10 minutes.

SERVES: 6 to 8

Adapted from a magazine

Fettuccine with Sausage

Submitted by Annette Gelber
Richmond, Virginia

INGREDIENTS:

8 ounces uncooked fettuccine
¼ cup butter
½ pound fresh mushrooms
1 clove garlic, minced
1 pound smoked sausage, sliced
     diagonally into ¼ inch pieces

2 eggs, beaten
½ cup heavy cream or half-and-half
1 cup grated Parmesan cheese
½ cup chopped fresh parsley

Melt butter in large skillet over medium heat. Slice mushrooms and add along with garlic. Cook and stir until mushrooms are soft. Remove from skillet; set aside. In same pan, heat sausage over medium heat until lightly browned. Drain any excess drippings. Meanwhile, cook fettuccine and keep warm. Return mushroom mixture to same skillet and keep warm.

In small bowl, combine eggs and cream. Add to skillet mixture; continuing heating just until cream mixture is hot but DO NOT BOIL. Add fettuccine, toss to combine. Mix in cheese and parsley. Serve immediately.

SERVES: 6

Favorite All Time Recipes

Linguini with White Clam Sauce

Submitted by Babs Jackson,
President/CEO, HHH

INGREDIENTS:

1 stick butter
3 tablespoons flour
4 cloves garlic, minced or pressed
2 cans chopped clams with liquid
2 small cans mushroom slices with liquid
1 cup water

½ cup chopped fresh parsley
Salt to taste
Cracked pepper to taste
1 pound linguini
½ cup grated Parmesan cheese

Melt butter in saucepan, add flour and minced garlic, and simmer for 2 minutes. Add clams, mushrooms, water, parsley, salt and pepper, and simmer for 20 minutes. Cook linguini according to directions and drain. Mix linguini with some of the sauce, pour onto large platter or bowl. Pour over remaining sauce. Sprinkle with Parmesan cheese.

SERVES: 4 to 6

Source unknown

Creamy Macaroni and Cheese

Submitted by St. James Youth Sunday School
Coles Point, Virginia

INGREDIENTS:

7 ounces elbow macaroni
2 cups cottage cheese
1 cup sour cream
1 egg, beaten

¾ teaspoon salt
Dash pepper
8 ounces grated sharp cheddar cheese

Preheat oven to 350° F. Cook elbow macaroni and drain. Combine cottage cheese, sour cream, egg, salt and pepper. Add cheese and mix well. Stir in elbow macaroni. Grease a medium-size casserole dish with cooking spray or shortening. Spoon combination into casserole dish and bake for 45 minutes.

SERVES: 10

Family recipe

Lasagne

Submitted by Dolly Hintz
Richmond, Virginia

INGREDIENTS:

1 pound pork or Italian sausage
1 pound ground beef
1 clove garlic, minced
1 tablespoon parsley flakes
1 tablespoon dried basil
1½ teaspoons salt
1 1-pound can tomatoes
2 6-ounce cans tomato paste

3 cups cream style cottage cheese
2 beaten eggs
2 teaspoons salt
3 tablespoons parsley flakes
½ teaspoon pepper
½ cup Parmesan cheese
1 pound mozzarella cheese, shredded
½ package lasagna noodles

Brown meat and pour off excess fat. Add garlic, parsley flakes, basil, salt, canned tomatoes and tomato paste. Simmer uncovered until sauce is thick, approximately 45 minutes to one hour.

Combine cottage cheese, eggs, salt, parsley flakes, pepper and Parmesan cheese. Cook the ½ package of noodles. Place half of noodles in 13×9×2 pan. Spread one-half cottage cheese mixture, one-half of mozzarella cheese and one-half meat sauce. Repeat layers. Bake 30 minutes at 375° F. Let stand 10 minutes before serving.

SERVES: 8 to 10

Family recipe

Pasta with Crabmeat and Herbs

Submitted by Annette Gelber
Richmond, Virginia

INGREDIENTS:

1 small onion, minced
1 carrot, shredded
1 clove garlic, minced
⅓ cup olive oil
3 tablespoons butter
6 ounces canned crabmeat, drained and
    flaked

½ cup chopped fresh basil or a teaspoon
    dried basil, crushed
2 tablespoons chopped parsley
1 tablespoon lemon juice
½ cup chopped pine nuts
½ teaspoon salt
½ package vermicelli, cooked and drained

Cook and stir onion, carrot and garlic in hot oil and butter in large skillet over medium-high heat until vegetables are tender, but not brown. Reduce heat to medium. Stir in crabmeat, basil, parsley and lemon juice, stirring constantly. Stir in pine nuts and salt. Remove from heat but keep warm. Cook vermicelli. Drain and place in large bowl. Pour sauce over; toss gently to coat.

Optional: Top with fresh, grated Parmesan cheese and parsley sprigs.

SERVES: 4

Adapted from a N.J. Department of Agriculture recipe

Texas Hash

Submitted by Winnie Ridill
Virginia Beach, Virginia

INGREDIENTS:

2–3 medium onions, sliced
1 green pepper, diced
3 tablespoons olive oil
¾ pound ground meat
1 pound can diced tomatoes

1 teaspoon chili powder
1 teaspoon salt
Dash of black pepper
2 cups noodles, uncooked

Saute onions and green peppers in oil until onions are yellow. Add ground meat and brown. Stir in tomatoes, chili powder, salt, black pepper, and noodles. Put in a greased (Pam will do) 1½ to 2 quart casserole dish. Bake at 350° F covered for 45 minutes. Remove lid and bake for 15 minutes more.

SERVES: 3 to 4

Family recipe

Vermicelli with Scallops

Submitted by Annette Gelber
Richmond, Virginia

INGREDIENTS:

1 pound bay scallops	1½ cups canned Italian tomatoes,
2 tablespoons fresh lemon juice	undrained and cut up
2 tablespoons chopped parsley	2 tablespoons chopped fresh basil or
1 onion, chopped	½ teaspoon dried, crushed basil
1 clove garlic, minced	½ teaspoon dried thyme leaves, crushed
2 tablespoons olive oil	2 tablespoons heavy cream
2 tablespoons butter, divided	Dash of ground nutmeg
	12 ounces cooked vermicelli

Rinse scallops and combine them in glass dish with lemon juice and chopped parsley. Cover and marinate in refrigerator while preparing sauce.

Cook and stir onion and garlic in oil and 1 tablespoon butter in large skillet over medium-high heat until onion is tender. Add tomatoes with juice, basil, oregano and thyme. Reduce heat to low. Cover; simmer 30 minutes, stirring occasionally. Meanwhile, cook vermicelli. Keep sauce and vermicelli warm in their own utensils.

Drain scallops; cook and stir in remaining 1 tablespoon butter in another large skillet over medium heat until scallops are cooked through and light golden brown on each side (about 10 minutes total), adding more butter if necessary. Add cream, nutmeg and tomato sauce mixture.

Place warm vermicelli in a large bowl and pour scallops and sauce over it. Toss gently to coat.

SERVES: 4

Adapted from a N.J. Department of Agriculture recipe

Chicken Spaghetti

Submitted by Elizabeth Burgess
And, South Carolina

INGREDIENTS:

4 cups cooked cubed chicken
3 cans (10¾ ounce each) cream mushroom
    soup, undiluted
2½ cups chicken broth
1 medium green pepper, chopped
1 medium onion, chopped
2 tablespoons dried parsley flakes

½ teaspoon salt
½ teaspoon pepper
1 pound process American cheese, cubed
1 package (12 ounce) spaghetti, cooked
    and drained
1 can (2¼ ounce) sliced ripe olives, optional

In a soup kettle or Dutch oven, combine chicken, soup, broth, pepper, onion, parsley, salt and pepper. Bring to a boil. Reduce heat, cover and simmer 15 to 20 minutes. Stir in cheese until melted. Add spaghetti and olives. Transfer to 2 greased 11 × 7 × 2-inch baking dishes. Cover and bake the casseroles at 325° F for 40 minutes. Uncover and bake 10 minutes longer.

Note: If desired, casserole can be covered tightly and frozen for up to three months. To use the frozen casserole: thaw in the refrigerator for 24 hours. Bake as directed.

SERVES: 12 to 16 (2 casseroles)

Taste of Home Magazine

Rice and Mushroom Casserole

Submitted by Lynn Wolf
Richmond, Virginia

INGREDIENTS:

3 medium onions, sliced
¼ pound butter
2 cups sliced mushrooms (fresh or canned)
1 cup converted rice (Uncle Ben's brand)

1 can consommé
1 cup water
Salt and pepper to taste

Sauté onions and sliced mushrooms in butter. Place in a casserole dish. Add consummé and water. Mix well with 1 cup Uncle Ben's converted rice. Bake at 350° F for 1½ hours. Stir occasionally. Cook covered. If there is still too much liquid after 1½ hours, continue to bake until it dries slightly.

SERVES: 8 to 10

Family recipe

Rice Pilaf (Armenian Style)

Submitted by Vicki Armentrout
Mechanicsville, Virginia

INGREDIENTS:

1 cup very fine noodles
1 cup rice (long grain)

2½ cups chicken broth
½ stick margarine

In a large pot, with a good fitting top, melt the margarine over medium-high heat. Add noodles, stirring until the noodles are brown. Careful that they don't burn! Add rice and chicken broth. Stir. Cook covered over low heat about 25 minutes. Add salt and pepper. Serve hot.

SERVES: 8

Family recipe

Vegetables

Sweet Potato, Pineapple and Cranberry Casserole

Submitted by Louis Mahoney
Richmond, Virginia

INGREDIENTS:

4 pounds sweet potatoes, canned, no syrup
or 4 pounds cooked fresh yams
1 can (20 ounce) crushed, no sugar added,
pineapple, drained

12 ounces fresh cranberries
½ teaspoon cinnamon
⅛ teaspoon allspice

If canned sweet potatoes without syrup are not available, use fresh yams and bake up to a day ahead and cool completely. Peel yams when cool.

Preheat oven to 325° F. Coat a non-stick lasagna pan with vegetable spray. If using canned potatoes, drain. Place drained canned potatoes or fresh peeled yams in pan. Mash with fork to flatten and cover bottom of pan. Spread drained, crushed pineapple evenly over potatoes or yams. Sprinkle on cinnamon and allspice. Rinse cranberries. Spread over top of casserole. Bake 45 minutes to an hour until heated through. Recipe can be prepared ahead, then baked before serving.

Note: Do not use canned sweet potatoes in syrup as it will make the dish too sweet.

SERVES: 12 to 16

Lois Paul

Roasted Vegetable Torte

Submitted by Elaine Evnen and Linda Braude
Lincoln, Nebraska

INGREDIENTS:

2 zucchini, cut into ¼-inch slices
1 red onion, cut in half lengthwise
    and sliced
1 teaspoon minced garlic
Good olive oil
Kosher salt
Freshly ground black pepper

2 red bell peppers, halved, cored, and
    seeded
2 yellow bell peppers, halved, cored and
    seeded
1 eggplant, unpeeled, cut into ¼-inch slices
    (1½ pounds)
½ cup freshly grated Parmesan cheese

Preheat the oven to 400° F.

Cook the zucchini, onions, garlic, and 2 tablespoons olive oil in a large sauté pan over medium heat for 10 minutes until the zucchini is tender. Season with salt and pepper. Brush the red and yellow peppers and eggplant with olive oil, season with salt and pepper, and roast on a baking sheet for 30 to 40 minutes, until soft but not browned.

In a 6-inch round cake pan, place each vegetable in a single, overlapping layer, sprinkling Parmesan cheese and salt and pepper to taste between each of the layers of vegetables. Begin with half of the eggplant, then layer half of the zucchini and onions, then all of the red peppers, then all of the yellow peppers, then the rest of the zucchini and onions, and finally the rest of the eggplant. Cover the top of the vegetables with a 6-inch round of parchment paper or waxed paper. Place a 6-inch flat disk (another cake plate or the bottom of a false-bottom tart pan) on top and weight it with a heavy jar. Place on a plate or baking sheet (it will leak) and chill completely. Drain the liquids, place on a platter, and serve at room temperature.

Note: Use red peppers to decorate top. To increase recipe, use more vegetables and a bigger spring form.

SERVES: 6

Adapted from *The Barefoot Contessa* cookbook

Vegetable Casserole

Submitted by Anise Lee Zimmerman
Richmond, Virginia

INGREDIENTS:

2 packages frozen broccoli
2 onions
2 cans small whole carrots

2 cans cream chicken soup, undiluted
1 stick sharp cheddar cheese
Bread crumbs

Pour boiling water over broccoli; drain, also drain other vegetables. Place vegetables in casserole. Melt cheese in soup. Cover with crumbs.

Bake casserole 1 hour 45 minutes at 375° F.

Note: Cheese soup may be used in place of the stick of sharp cheddar. Do not put any water in the cream of chicken soup or cheese soup.

This casserole may be prepared the day before you plan to bake.

SERVES: 12

Family recipe

Escalloped Asparagus

Submitted by Polly W. Boaz
Keysville, Virginia

INGREDIENTS:

6 eggs, hard boiled and peeled
2 cans asparagus spears, drain and save
   liquid

4 thin slices of cheese
1 tablespoon flour

Boil eggs, peel, and set aside. Drain the asparagus, saving the liquid to make a sauce.

Place asparagus spears in baking dish, slice eggs and place on top of asparagus. Grate or cut slices of cheese. Spread on asparagus. Make a white sauce with flour and liquid from asparagus cans. Bake at 350° F for ingredients to mix.

SERVES: 6 to 8

Family recipe

Asparagus Casserole

Submitted by Madeline Campbell
Richmond, Virginia

INGREDIENTS:

2 large cans asparagus, drained
Bread slices, crust removed
1 large can green peas, drained
1 large can water chestnuts

2 eggs
1 can cream of mushroom soup
1 cup grated sharp cheese

Butter casserole dish. Line dish with bread (crust removed). Place asparagus (drained) on top of bread. Pour over one large can of LeSueur peas, drained. Add one can of sliced water chestnuts. Two hard boiled eggs sliced. One can cream of mushroom soup, mixed with ½ cup liquid from asparagus. Salt and pepper to taste. Sprinkle with one cup grated sharp cheese. Top with buttered bread (crust cut off). Bake at 300° for approximately 45 minutes.

SERVES: 8

Family recipe

Asparagus Casserole with Almonds

Submitted by Lorraine Moody
Chester, Virginia

INGREDIENTS:

¼ pound sharp cheese, grated
1 small can mushrooms
1 4-ounce can mushroom soup
½ cup fine bread crumbs

2 cups asparagus, drained and cut
4 hard boiled eggs, grated
1 cup salted almonds, chopped

Add cheese and mushrooms to soup. Sprinkle bread crumbs in greased casserole dish. Place a layer of asparagus, layer of eggs, layer of almonds. Repeat until dish is filled. Cover with soup mixture. Sprinkle top with crumbs. Dot with butter. Bake at 400° F for 15 to 20 minutes or until hot.

SERVES: 8

Family recipe

Broccoli Casserole

Submitted by Elizabeth Jordan
Gloucester Point, Virginia

INGREDIENTS:

2 10-ounce packages frozen broccoli florets	1 egg, slightly beaten
½ cup mayonnaise	1½ cups shredded mild cheddar cheese
1 tablespoon minced onion	½ cup herb stuffing
1 can cream of mushroom soup	½ cup melted butter

Cook broccoli according to package directions; drain. Combine mayonnaise, onion, soup, egg and cheese. Add broccoli. Stir with wooden spoon. Place mixture in 1 quart casserole dish (9×9 square baking dish). Gently stir stuffing mix and butter with a fork in a small bowl. Sprinkle on top of broccoli mixture. Bake at 350° F for approximately 35 minutes.

SERVES: 6

Family recipe

Candied Carrots

Submitted by Mikki Perri Jacques
Virginia Beach, Virginia

INGREDIENTS:

5 medium carrots	2 tablespoons light brown sugar
¼ cup butter	½ teaspoon salt
¼ cup canned jellied cranberry sauce	

Scrape carrots and slice crosswise ½-inch thick (or into rounds). Cook, covered, in small amount of boiling water, until just tender, 6 to 10 minutes.

Combine butter, cranberry sauce, brown sugar and salt in a skillet. Heat slowly and stir until cranberry sauce melts. Add drained carrots; heat, stirring occasionally, until nicely glazed on all sides, about 5 minutes.

SERVES: 4

Source unknown

Cabbage Au Gratin

Submitted by Miriam Pendleton
Richmond, Virginia

INGREDIENTS:

6 cups finely sliced cabbage (1 medium head)
4 cups boiling water
1 teaspoon salt
4 tablespoons butter
4 tablespoons flour

2 cups milk
¼ teaspoon white pepper
6 slices American cheese
½ cup plain bread crumbs
6 tablespoons bacon bits

Add salt to boiling water. Add cabbage. Cook on high heat 8 minutes until crisp tender. Do not overcook. Drain well. Place in greased casserole.

Melt butter slowly. Add flour and cook 1 minute until bubbles come. Slowly add milk. Stir constantly until thickened. Add salt and white pepper. Pour over cabbage. Add cheese slices to cover. Add bread crumbs and bacon bits. Bake 15 to 20 minutes until bubbly at 350° F.

This casserole may be made ahead until the cheese is to be added. Press plastic wrap on top of sauce topping and refrigerate. To complete dish, bring to room temperature, remove plastic covering and add cheese slices, bread crumbs, and bacon bits. Place in pre-heated oven and bake.

SERVES: 6 to 8

Source unknown

Carrot Squash Casserole

Submitted by Barbara T. Lester
Richmond, Virginia

INGREDIENTS:

1 8-ounce container sour cream
2 cups cooked, cooled mashed yellow
   squash
1 medium onion, chopped
1 10-ounce can cream of chicken soup
¾ cup grated carrots

1 cup milk
½ cup melted margarine
1 8-ounce package herb stuffing mix
2 eggs, beaten
1 cup grated sharp cheddar cheese

Mix all ingredients in a bowl. Preheat oven to 350° F. Lightly grease baking dish. Pour ingredients into baking dish and bake for 45 minutes.

SERVES: 6 to 8

Family recipe

Whiskey Corn Pudding

Submitted by Maryglyn McGraw
Richmond, Virginia

INGREDIENTS:

1 10-ounce package frozen corn, cooked
   and drained
1 tablespoon cornstarch
1 cup milk, divided
3 tablespoons bourbon whiskey

3 tablespoons sugar
1 egg, beaten
Salt and pepper to taste
3 tablespoons butter, melted

Whisk cornstarch and milk until smooth. Add and whisk whiskey, sugar, salt and pepper. Add melted butter. Whisk in eggs. Blend with corn. Place in greased 1½ quart casserole. Bake in 350° F oven until firm in center, 45 to 50 minutes.

SERVES: 6 to 8

Friend

Holiday Celery Dish

Submitted by Pat Glupker
Richmond, Virginia

INGREDIENTS:

6 cups diagonally sliced celery, ¾" thick
1 cup hot water
1 teaspoon chicken seasoned base
¼ cup butter
¼ cup flour
½ teaspoon salt

⅛ teaspoon pepper
1 cup milk
3 green onions, sliced
2 tablespoons chopped pimento
Chinese crisp noodles

Cook celery in water with chicken base for 5 minutes. Drain and save liquid (if necessary, add water to make 1 cup). Make white sauce with butter, flour, salt, pepper milk and saved cooking water. Add celery, green onions and pimento to sauce and pour into shallow baking dish. Top with crisp noodles and bake 15 minutes at 350° F.

SERVES: 6

Family recipe

Smothered Onion Pie

Submitted by Laura R. Siff
Richmond, Virginia

INGREDIENTS:

1 9" prepared pie shell
4 tablespoons butter
2–3 large onions
2 leeks
½ cup minced parsley

2 eggs
¾ cup sour cream
Salt and pepper to taste
1 cup fine bread crumbs
⅓ cup chopped walnuts

Slice onions and leeks and sauté in 3 tablespoons butter. Cook until translucent. Beat eggs with sour cream and parsley and salt and pepper. Pour into pie shell. Make buttered bread crumbs with walnuts. Sprinkle on top of pie and bake 25 to 30 minutes in 375° F oven.

SERVES: 6

Family recipe

Sicilian Caponata

Submitted by Karen Shea
Richmond, Virginia

INGREDIENTS:

1 eggplant
Salt
½ cup olive oil
1 onion, sliced
2 sweet red peppers, cored, seeded and
    cut into 1 inch pieces
2 sticks celery, sliced

1 pound canned plum tomatoes
2 tablespoons red wine vinegar
1 tablespoon sugar
1 clove garlic, crushed
12 black olives, pitted
1 tablespoon capers
Salt and pepper

Cut the eggplant in half and score the cut surface. Sprinkle with salt and leave to drain in a colander or on paper towels for 30 minutes. Rinse, pat dry and cut into one inch cubes. Heat the oil in a large sauté pan and add the onion, peppers and celery. Lower the heat and cook for about 5 minutes, stirring occasionally. Add the eggplant and cook 5 more minutes. Sieve the tomatoes to remove the seeds and add the pulp and liquid to the vegetables in the sauté pan. Add the remaining ingredients except the olives and capers and cook for 2 more minutes. Slice the olives in quarters and add to the vegetables with the capers. Simmer, uncovered, over moderate heat for 15 minutes to evaporate most of the liquid. Adjust the seasoning and serve hot or cold.

SERVES: 6

Adapted from *Italian Cooking*

Scolloped Potatoes with Cheese

Submitted by Brenda Morris
Hamburg, New Jersey

INGREDIENTS:

1 garlic clove, halved
Cooking spray
6 red potatoes, peeled and sliced
2 tablespoons butter, melted

½ teaspoon salt
⅛ teaspoon black pepper
½ cup shredded Gruyère cheese
1 cup fat free milk

Preheat oven to 425° F. Rub an 11×7 baking dish with garlic. Discard garlic. Coat dish with cooking spray. Arrange half of potatoes in dish. Drizzle with half of the butter. Sprinkle with half of salt and half of pepper. Top with half of cheese. Repeat layers.

Bring milk to a boil, pour over potato mixture. Bake 40 minutes or until tender.

SERVES: 6

Family recipe

Easy Potato Casserole

Submitted by Jennie Fritz
Richmond, Virginia

INGREDIENTS:

1 (32 ounce) package shredded hash
    brown potatoes, thawed
1 medium onion, chopped
½ cup chopped green pepper
1 can cream of potato soup, undiluted
1 can cream of celery soup, undiluted

8 ounces sour cream
½ teaspoon salt
⅛ teaspoon pepper
1 cup (4 ounces) shredded Monterey
    Jack cheese

Combine all except cheese. Stir well. Turn into greased shallow 2 quart casserole.

Bake 325° F oven for 1 hour and 15 minutes.

Sprinkle with cheese and bake an additional 15 minutes.

SERVES: 8+

Source unknown

Potatoes with Artichokes and Olives

Submitted by Deanne Mountcastle
Richmond, Virginia

INGREDIENTS:

2 9-ounce packages frozen artichoke hearts
2 tablespoons fresh lemon juice
1 pound red potatoes, cut in chunks
2 cups fat-free chicken broth
2 tablespoons olive oil

1 small onion thinly sliced
½ cup sliced Kalamata olives
1 teaspoon drained capers
Salt and pepper to taste
Freshly ground Parmesan cheese (optional)

In a large bowl, place artichokes and lemon juice. Add enough water to cover artichokes. Let stand until artichokes are thawed; drain well. In a 3-quart saucepan, combine potatoes and chicken broth; add enough water to cover potatoes. Bring to a boil, reduce heat and simmer 10 minutes or until tender; drain. In a large nonstick skillet, heat oil over medium-high heat. Cook onion 5 minutes or until tender, stirring occasionally. Reduce heat to medium; stir in artichokes, potatoes, olives and capers. Cook, uncovered, about 5 minutes, stirring frequently, until hot. Season to taste with salt and pepper. If desired, sprinkle with cheese.

SERVES: 8

Source unknown

Big and Easy Potato Casserole
Submitted by Bernice Carter
Richmond, Virginia

INGREDIENTS:

2 pound bag hashbrowns, thawed
¼ cup margarine, melted
1 teaspoon salt and pepper
2 tablespoons minced onion

1 can cream of chicken soup
1 8-ounce sour cream
2 cups grated sharp cheese

Grease a 9 × 13 × 2 inch pan. Put potatoes in a large bowl and pour on margarine. Mix rest of ingredients and combine with potatoes. Put in pan and bake at 350° F for 1 hour.

SERVES: 8–10

Family recipe

Twice Baked Stuffed Potatoes

Submitted by Jean Goldman
Richmond, Virginia

INGREDIENTS:

6 baking potatoes (large size)
4 ounces sour cream
6 ounces extra sharp cheddar cheese,
    grated, divided

½ stick butter or margarine, melted
Salt and pepper to taste

Bake potatoes until done (about 1 hour at 375° F). Be sure they're soft all the way through. Cut each potato in half lengthwise. Carefully scoop out potato from shells. Place scooped-out potatoes in large mixing bowl. Add melted butter (or margarine), sour cream, ½ of shredded cheese, salt and pepper. Beat (either by mashing or using electric mixer) until creamy. Season to taste, adding more sour cream, cheese, salt or/and pepper, if needed.

Fill each ½ of potato shell with potato mixture. Top each half with a sprinkling of the remaining cheddar cheese. At this point, you may refrigerate or freeze until ready to heat. Heat on cookie sheet for about 20 to 25 minutes at 350° F until bubbly and hot.

Note: If you freeze potatoes, defrost before heating.

SERVES: 12

Cooking class

Spinach Casserole

Submitted by Jean Goldman
Richmond, Virginia

INGREDIENTS:

4 packages (10 ounces each) frozen
    chopped spinach, well drained
1½ cups grated sharp cheddar cheese,
    reduced fat variety
1 cup sour cream, fat free

1 can cream of mushroom soup, 98%
    fat free
1 package dried onion soup mix
1 teaspoon garlic powder

Mix all ingredients together well. Place in 11″×8″×2″ casserole. Bake uncovered at 325° F for 30 to 40 minutes.

SERVES: 10

Family recipe

Scalloped Spinach

Submitted by Laura Siff
Richmond, Virginia

INGREDIENTS:

2 10-ounce packages frozen spinach
¾ cup milk
¾ cup shredded cheddar cheese
3 beaten eggs

3 tablespoons chopped onion
1 cup coarse bread crumbs
1 tablespoon butter, melted

Cook spinach; drain well. Mix milk, ½ cup of cheese, eggs, onion, ½ teaspoon salt, a dash of pepper. Turn into greased 8×8×2 inch pan. Bake 350° F for 25 minutes. Combine crumbs, remaining cheese and butter; sprinkle atop spinach mixture. Bake until knife inserted comes out clean, 10 to 15 minutes more. Let stand 5 minutes.

SERVES: 6

Adapted from *Better Homes & Gardens Cookbook* (1952)

Creamy Spinach Bake

Submitted by Kate Yoffy
Richmond, Virginia

INGREDIENTS:

4 slices bacon
2 (10 ounce) packages frozen chopped
spinach, thawed and well drained

1½ cups sour cream
1 (.25 ounce) envelope dry onion soup mix
⅓ cup grated Parmesan cheese

Fry bacon until crisp, drain on paper towels, crumble, and set aside.

Combine spinach, sour cream, and dry soup mix. Stir well. Spoon mixture into a lightly greased one quart casserole dish. Sprinkle Parmesan cheese on top of the spinach mixture.

Bake at 350° F for 30 minutes. Top with bacon and serve.

SERVES: 4

Source unknown

Sweet Potato Souffle

Submitted by Mikki Perri Jacques
Virginia Beach, Virginia

SOUFFLE INGREDIENTS:

3 cups cooked, mashed sweet potatoes
1 cup sugar
½ teaspoon salt
2 eggs, beaten

½ stick margarine, melted
½ cup sweet milk
1 teaspoon vanilla

Mix all ingredients, pour into greased baking dish, and cover with topping.

TOPPING INGREDIENTS:

1 cup brown sugar
⅓ cup flour

1 cup chopped nuts
⅓ stick margarine

Melt margarine and stir in nuts, flour, and sugar. Sprinkle over sweet potatoes and bake in glass Pyrex dish at 325° F oven 45 to 50 minutes.

SERVES: 15+

Family recipe

Sweet Potatoes in Orange Shells

Submitted by Ann Bendheim
Richmond, Virginia

INGREDIENTS:

3 pounds sweet potatoes, cooked and
    mashed (about 6 cups)
2 eggs
¾ cup brown sugar
½ cup melted butter
½ teaspoon cinnamon

1 teaspoon salt
1 cup pecans, finely ground
Fresh orange juice (up to 1 cup)
8 large orange shells
Miniature marshmallows (optional)

Place sweet potatoes in a mixing bowl. Beat in eggs, melted butter, brown sugar, cinnamon, salt and pecans. Add the orange juice only if the sweet potatoes seem dry. Fill orange shells with sweet potatoes; refrigerate until ready to use. Bake at 375° F for 20 minutes, or until heated through. Place marshmallows on top; place under the broiler until nicely browned. (To make orange shells, slice off tops of oranges and remove pulp.)

SERVES: 8

Adapted from *Soupcon Cookbook*

Savory Summer Pie

Submitted by Judy Harrell
Richmond, Virginia

INGREDIENTS:

3 refrigerated pie crusts
½ large sweet onion, chopped
2 garlic cloves, minced
(Up to 1 cup of other chopped fresh
veggies can be added, e.g., red or
green pepper, squash)
2 tablespoons olive oil
2 tablespoons chopped fresh basil (I use
about 8 large leaves)
4 large eggs

2 cups half-and-half
1 teaspoon salt
½ teaspoon pepper
2 cups shredded Monterey Jack cheese
⅓ cup shredded Parmesan cheese
3 small tomatoes, cut into ¼" thick slices

Fit pie crust into a 9-inch deep-dish quiche or tart pan, turning under any excess crust on edges; prick bottom and sides of pie crust with a fork.

Bake at 425° F for 10 minutes. Remove from oven; set aside. Reset oven temperature to 375° F.

Sauté onion, garlic (and any other chopped veggies) in hot oil in medium skillet 5 minutes or until tender; stir in basil.

Whisk together eggs and next 3 ingredients in a large bowl; stir in sautéed vegetables and cheeses. Pour into crust; cover top with tomato slices.

Bake at 375° F for 50 minutes or until set. Let stand 5 minutes before serving. Refrigerate leftovers and serve chilled or warmed in microwave.

SERVES: 6

Adapted from *Southern Living*

Baked Tomatoes Italiano

Submitted by Nancy G. Powell
Richmond, Virginia

INGREDIENTS:

4 large tomatoes, ripe but firm
1 tablespoon olive oil
3 cloves garlic, minced
⅔ cup dried bread crumbs
2 tablespoons fresh basil (2 teaspoons dried)

2 tablespoons fresh oregano (½ teaspoon dried)
2 tablespoons green onion, minced
½ cup Parmesan cheese

Grease shallow baking pan. Core tomatoes, cut in half. Lightly salt; turn over on paper towel to drain. Heat oil in skillet. Add garlic and saute 1 to 2 minutes. DO NOT SCORCH. Add crumbs, cook 2 minutes more, stirring constantly. Add herbs and onion, cook 30 seconds. Remove from heat, stir in cheese. Put tomatoes in baking pan and top with crumb mixture. Bake 15 to 20 minutes until tomatoes just lose firmness. Serve immediately.

SERVES: 8

Family recipe

Southern Tomato Pie

Submitted by Connie Babb
Richmond, Virginia

INGREDIENTS:

2 pie crusts
½ cup mayonnaise
2 cups shredded cheddar cheese
½ cup chopped onion
3 peeled tomatoes, thinly sliced

6 or 8 chopped fresh basil leaves or ½ teaspoon dried basil
20 Ritz crackers, crushed
2 teaspoons butter, softened

Brown two pie crusts in 400° F oven. Mix together mayonnaise, cheese, onion, and basil. Spread thin layer of mixture on bottom of pie crust.

Place tomatoes on a paper towel to drain. Place tomatoes on top of first layer of mixture and top with crushed Ritz crackers mixed with 2 teaspoons of butter. Put foil on top of pies, put on cookie sheet and bake at 350° F for 40 minutes. Remove the foil for the last 5 minutes of cooking time.

SERVES: 12–16

Source unknown

Zucchini Casserole

Submitted by Bernice Bock
Richmond, Virginia

INGREDIENTS:

4 medium zucchini, sliced ½" thick
¾ cup shredded carrots
½ cup chopped onions
6 tablespoons butter or margarine, divided

½ cup cubed cheese
½ cup sour cream
2½ cups herbed croutons, divided
1 can cream of chicken soup

Cook zucchini in boiling salted water. Drain. In saucepan, saute until tender, carrots, onions and 4 tablespoons butter. Remove from heat. Stir in 1½ cups croutons, soup, sour cream and cheese. Gently add zucchini to mixture. Turn into 1½ quart greased casserole. Melt remaining butter, add rest of croutons, 1 cup, and toss lightly. Sprinkle over casserole. Bake at 350° F for 30 to 40 minutes.

SERVES: 12

Adapted from *Pathwork of Hillendale's Family Favorites* (1975)

Breads

Pineapple Pizza

Submitted by Annette Gelber
Richmond, Virginia

INGREDIENTS:

2 cans (8 ounces each) crushed pineapple
½ cup bottled pizza sauce
1 clove garlic, pressed
1 teaspoon dried oregano, crumbled
½ loaf frozen bread dough, thawed
½ pound Italian sausage, crumbled, cooked

1 small green bell pepper, seeded and
  sliced
¼ cup chopped green onion
2 cups shredded mozzarella cheese
2 tablespoons grated Parmesan cheese

Preheat oven to 500° F. Drain pineapple well, pressing out excess juice with back of spoon. In small bowl, combine pizza sauce, garlic and oregano. Roll and stretch thawed dough to fit greased 12 inch pizza pan. Spread dough with pizza sauce mixture. Top with sausage, green pepper, onion, pineapple and cheese. Bake in preheated oven 12 to 15 minutes or until pizza is bubbly and crust is browned.

SERVES: 4

Adapted from *Dole Food Co. Cookbook*

Yeast Rolls
Submitted by Elizabeth L. Critz
Richmond, Virginia

INGREDIENTS:

2 cups hot water
1 teaspoon salt
½ cup sugar
3 tablespoons liquid shortening

1 cake yeast
7 cups flour, divided
1 egg

Place water, salt, sugar and shortening in large bowl. Cool to lukewarm, then add yeast and dissolve. Stir in 3 cups of flour. Add egg. Gradually add the remaining flour, adding only enough to make a soft dough. Knead until smooth and not sticky. Place dough into large greased bowl and grease top. Let rise double in bulk. Punch down, shape into rolls or loaves. Let rise again until doubled in size. Bake rolls at 425° F for 20 minutes, loaves at 400° F for 30 minutes. You may use less sugar or not any.

YIELDS: 2 dozen rolls

Family recipe

Sixty-Minute Rolls
Submitted by Karen Comer
Richmond, Virginia

INGREDIENTS:

3½ to 4½ cups flour
3 tablespoons sugar
1 teaspoon salt
2 packages yeast

1 cup milk
½ cup water
¼ cup margarine

In large bowl, thoroughly mix 1½ cups flour, sugar, salt and yeast.

Combine milk, water and margarine in a saucepan. Heat over low heat until liquids are very warm (120–130° F). Margarine does not need to melt. Gradually add to dry ingredients and beat 2 minutes at medium speed of electric mixer, scraping bowl occasionally. Stir in enough additional flour to make a soft dough. Turn out onto lightly floured board; knead until smooth and elastic, about 5 minutes. Place in greased bowl, turning to grease top. Cover; place bowl in pan of warm water. Let rise 15 minutes. Turn dough out onto floured board. Divide in half and shape as rolls. Cover and let rise in warm place, free from draft for 15 minutes. Bake at 425° F about 12 minutes or until done. Remove from baking sheets and cool on wire racks.

YIELDS: 24 rolls

Fleishmann's Yeast Book

Zucchini Sweet Bread

Submitted by Vanessa McPherson
Virginia Beach, Virginia

INGREDIENTS:

3 eggs
¾ cup oil
2 cups sugar
2 teaspoons vanilla
2 cups shredded zucchini
½ cup applesauce
½ cup raisins

1 cup chopped nuts
3 cups flour
1 teaspoon salt
1 teaspoon baking soda
1 teaspoon baking powder
2 teaspoons cinnamon
1 teaspoon nutmeg

Preheat oven to 350° F.

Sift together flour, salt, baking soda, baking powder, cinnamon and nutmeg. Set aside.

Mix well eggs, oil, sugar, vanilla, zucchini, applesauce. Add raisins and nuts.

Combine all of the ingredients and mix thoroughly. Pour into 2 greased loaf pans. Bake for 1 hour.

SERVES: 20 to 24

Family recipe

Corn Bread

Submitted by Gerry Herring
Richmond, Virginia

INGREDIENTS:

2 boxes Jiffy Corn Muffin Mix
1 can cream style corn
1 stick butter, melted

3 eggs, beaten
16 ounces sour cream

Mix all ingredients together. Pour into large greased baking dish. (Larger dish 12″×9″×2″) Bake at 350° F for 45 minutes or until golden brown.

SERVES: 12

Family recipe

Vienna Bread

Submitted by Babs Jackson
President/CEO, HHH
Richmond, Virginia

INGREDIENTS:

1 loaf Vienna bread or Italian bread
Sliced Swiss cheese (enough to fill
    bread slices)

FROSTING INGREDIENTS:

½ teaspoon softened butter or margarine   2 teaspoons poppy seeds
2 teaspoons dry mustard

Preheat oven to 350° F. Cut off the top crust and sides of the bread. Trim without taking too much of the bread. Slice into 1½ inch, or wider, sections, but do not cut through the bottom. Put a slice of Swiss cheese inside each section. Place bread in a foil "boat". Combine butter, mustard and poppy seeds to frost top and sides of loaf. Bake uncovered for 20 to 25 minutes. Will get slightly brown.

YIELDS: 1 loaf

Friend — Barb Oakley

Yeast Bread

Submitted by Ruth B. Stanley
Church Road, Virginia

INGREDIENTS:

4 teaspoons dry yeast   4 teaspoons salt
1 cup lukewarm water   4 tablespoons sugar
3 cups lukewarm liquid (water, milk   4 tablespoons melted shortening
    or both)   About 12 cups of flour

Mix yeast in the cup of lukewarm water, stir and let stand 5 minutes. Meanwhile, measure remaining liquid into a large bowl; add salt and sugar, then stir in yeast and 2 cups flour; stir, then add shortening and rest of flour. Mix well and knead into a medium firm dough. Brush with shortening; cover and set bowl in a pan of very warm water. Let rise double in bulk (1 hour). Punch it down and let rise again, 20 to 30 minutes. Knead down. Divide into 3 or 4 portions and place in greased loaf pans. Let rise in a warm place until double in bulk. Bake in oven at 350° F for 15 to 20 minutes.

YIELDS: 3 large loaves or 1 loaf and 4 dozen rolls

Family recipe

Apple Bread

Submitted by Maria Romhilt
Richmond, Virginia

INGREDIENTS:

2 sticks sweet butter
2 cups sugar
2 teaspoons cinnamon
4 eggs
4 tablespoons milk
2 teaspoons vanilla

4 apples, peeled and chopped
4 cups flour
½ teaspoon salt
½ teaspoon baking soda
4 teaspoons baking powder

Beat softened butter well. Add cinnamon to sugar and beat with butter until fluffy. Add eggs, milk and vanilla and beat. Add apples and mix. Mix together flour, salt and baking powder and soda. Add and mix until blended. Put batter in 2 loaf pans which are well greased. Bake at 350° F for 50 to 55 minutes. Cool for 15 minutes and then remove from pans. Pour Glaze over warm loaves.

GLAZE INGREDIENTS:

1 cup powdered sugar
1 teaspoon cinnamon

4 tablespoons sweet butter
2 tablespoons water

Mix cinnamon and sugar. Melt butter and add water. Add butter to sugar mixture and mix until smooth.

Note: Apple bread freezes well.

YIELDS: 2 loaves

Adapted from *Stuffed Cougar*

Willa's Banana Bread

Submitted by Kathy Burns
Richmond, Virginia

INGREDIENTS:

1½ cups sugar
½ cup Crisco oil
2–3 eggs (depending on size)
1½ cups mashed banana (can substitute
    pumpkin or combine both to equal
    1½ cups)

⅓ cup water
1¾ cups flour
1 teaspoon baking soda
1 teaspoon baking powder
1 teaspoon salt
¾ teaspoon cinnamon

Mix sugar, oil, eggs, banana and water. Add flour, baking soda, baking powder, salt and cinnamon. Mix well. Pour into greased and floured loaf pan. Bake one hour or until knife comes out clean.

Note: Can be doubled. If desired, 1 cup raisins and/or ¾ cup chopped pecans can be added.

YIELDS: 1 loaf

Family recipe

Pineapple-Carrot Bread

Submitted by Willoughby Adams
Richmond, Virginia

INGREDIENTS:

3 cups flour
2 cups sugar
2 cups shredded carrots
1 8-ounce can crushed pineapple,
    undrained

1½ cups vegetable oil
3 eggs
1 teaspoon baking soda
1 tablespoon cinnamon
1 teaspoon salt

Combine ingredient. Pour batter into 2 loaf pans (6 to 8 mini-loaf pans). Bake 45 to 60 minutes at 325° F until a toothpick inserted in center, comes out clean.

Note: These freeze beautifully!

YIELDS: 2 loaves

Source unknown

Lemon Poppy Seed Bread

Submitted by Pat Glupker
Richmond, Virginia

INGREDIENTS:

½ cup butter
1 cup sugar
2 eggs
1½ cups flour
1 teaspoon baking powder
¼ teaspoon salt

1 teaspoon lemon zest
2 tablespoons poppy seeds
½ cup milk
Topping:
¼ cup sugar
¼ cup lemon juice

Cream butter and sugar until light; beat in eggs, one at a time. Combine flour, baking powder, salt, lemon zest and poppy seed and add to the egg mixture alternately with the milk. Bake in a well buttered loaf pan 50 to 60 minutes at 350° F. After baking and while still warm and in the pan, poke bread all over with small skewer. Stir together the ¼ cup sugar and lemon juice and pour over hot bread. Let cool.

YIELD: 1 Loaf

Original recipe

Pumpkin Bread

Submitted by Hazel (Sunny) Cliff
Fredericksburg, Virginia

INGREDIENTS:

5 eggs
1¼ cups vegetable oil
1 can solid-pack pumpkin (15 ounces)
2 cups all purpose flour
2 cups sugar

2 3-ounce each cook and serve vanilla
pudding mix
1 teaspoon baking soda
1 teaspoon ground cinnamon
½ teaspoon salt

In a mixing bowl, beat eggs. Add oil and pumpkin; beat until smooth. Combine remaining ingredients; gradually beat into pumpkin mixture. Pour batter into five greased 5″×2½″×2″ loaf pans.

Bake at 325° F for 50 to 55 minutes or until toothpick inserted near the center comes out clean. Cool on wire racks.

Note: May also be baked in two greased 8″×4″×2″ loaf pans for 75 to 80 minutes.

YIELDS: 5 miniature loaves or 2 large loaves

Taste of Home cookbook

Thin Mandel Bread

Submitted by Babs Jackson,
President/CEO, HHH

INGREDIENTS:

2 cups flour	4 eggs
1 stick margarine	½ teaspoon salt
1¼ cups sugar	½ teaspoon baking powder
3 cups pecan halves	2 teaspoons vanilla
½ cup sliced almonds	

Cream margarine and sugar. Add eggs, one at a time. Add dry ingredients, vanilla, then nuts. Put in 3 Pam-sprayed or greased metal ice cube trays or 3 foil pans (greased or sprayed) 8″×5″×1″. Bake at 350° for 30 to 35 minutes. Cool, invert to remove from pans, then put back in pans and freeze.

Remove from freezer and slice very thin. Lay on ungreased cookie sheet. Sprinkle with cinnamon and sugar mixture. Bake 8 to 10 minutes until lightly browned. Remove from pan immediately.

YIELD: Several dozen

Family recipe

Angel Biscuits

Submitted by Patty Giles
Richmond, Virginia

INGREDIENTS:

1 package yeast	3 teaspoons baking powder
¼ cup warm water	1 cup vegetable shortening
5 cups all-purpose flour	¼ cup sugar
1 teaspoon baking soda	2 cups buttermilk
1 teaspoon salt	

Dissolve yeast in ¼ cup lukewarm water. Sift flour, baking soda, salt, baking powder and sugar together. Cut in shortening. Add yeast, water and buttermilk. Mix well. Cover and refrigerate 2 hours or overnight.

Heat oven to 400° F. Roll out dough to ½-inch thickness on floured surface. Cut with a 2-inch biscuit cutter. Place on ungreased baking sheet and bake until lightly browned — 10 to 15 minutes.

YIELDS: 3 to 4 dozen

Family recipe

Cheddar Garlic Biscuits

Submitted by Sandra Sabo
Emporia, Virginia

INGREDIENTS:

2 cups Bisquick
⅔ cup milk
½ cup shredded cheddar cheese

2 tablespoons butter
⅛ teaspoon garlic powder

Heat oven to 450° F. Mix Bisquick, milk and cheese to form a soft dough. Drop by tablespoons onto ungreased cookie sheet—about 9 spoonfuls. Bake 8 to 10 minutes. Mix butter and garlic powder. Brush over warm biscuits.

SERVES: 4 to 5

Bisquick recipe

Biscuits

Submitted by Barbara T. Lester, MD
Richmond, Virginia

INGREDIENTS:

2 cups self rising flour
½ cup shortening (I use Crisco)

¾ cup milk
⅛ teaspoon salt

Measure flour into bowl. Add salt. Cut shortening into flour until mix looks like meal. Pour in most of milk to make dough soft and pliable, almost sticky. Knead lightly 25 times or so. Pat or roll on flour-covered cloth or board to ½ inch thickness. Cut into rounds with flour covered drinking glass (brim of glass flour covered) or biscuit cutter.

Bake at 450° F for 10 minutes or until golden brown.

SERVES: 6 to 8

Family recipe

Morning Glory Muffins

Submitted by Nancy G. Powell
Richmond, Virginia

INGREDIENTS:

2½ cups sugar
4 cups all-purpose flour
4 teaspoons baking soda
4 teaspoons cinnamon
1 teaspoon salt
4 cups carrots, grated
1 cup raisins

1 cup pecans, chopped
1 cup sweetened chopped coconut
2 apples, peeled and grated
6 eggs
2 cups vegetable oil
4 teaspoons vanilla

Preheat oven to 350° F. Sift together sugar, flour, baking soda, cinnamon and salt. Stir in carrots, raisins, pecans, coconut and apples. Beat eggs with oil and vanilla. Stir into flour mixture until just combined. Spoon batter into well-greased muffin tins, filling to top. Bake 35 minutes or until springy to the touch. Moist and yummy! *Note:* This recipe may be halved.

YIELDS: 30 muffins

Mennonites

Breakfast Muffins

Submitted by Mae Williams
Ports, Virginia

INGREDIENTS:

2 cups Martha White self-rising flour
1 egg

2 heaping tablespoons Dukes mayonnaise
1 cup milk

Preheat oven to 400° F. Grease 12-cup muffin tin. Stir all ingredients together with a spoon. Spoon batter into muffin tin. Bake until lightly browned and test for doneness.

SERVES: 12

Original recipe

Blueberry Muffins

Submitted by Winnie Ridill
Virginia Beach, Virginia

INGREDIENTS:

1½ cups flour
⅔ teaspoon salt
3 teaspoons baking powder
¾ cup sugar

⅔ cup milk
1 egg
¼ cup melted butter or margarine
1 cup blueberries

Preheat oven to 400° F. Mix flour, salt and baking powder. Add sugar and stir. Add milk, eggs and melted butter. Beat until smooth. Fold in blueberries. Put into greased muffin tin (Pam works fine) or into paper baking cups, (about ⅔ full). Sprinkle tops with a little cinnamon sugar. Bake at 400° F for 20 to 25 minutes.

YIELDS: 12 muffins

Family recipe

Banana Chocolate Chip Muffins

Submitted by Cathy B. Hinton
Midlothian, Virginia

INGREDIENTS:

1½ cups all purpose flour
⅔ cup sugar
1½ teaspoons baking powder
¼ teaspoon salt
1 cup mashed ripe bananas (about 2 large)

1 large egg
½ cup (1 stick) unsalted butter, melted
¼ cup milk
¾ cup mini semisweet chocolate chips

Preheat oven to 350° F. Line twelve ⅓ cup muffin cups with muffin liners. Mix flour, sugar, baking powder and salt in large bowl. Mix mashed bananas, egg, melted butter and milk in medium bowl. Stir banana mixture into dry ingredients just until blended (do not overmix). Stir in chocolate chips.

Divide batter among prepared muffin cups, filling each about ¾ full. Bake muffins until tops are pale golden and tester inserted into center comes out with some melted chocolate attached but no crumbs, about 20 to 24 minutes. Transfer muffins to rack; cool.

YIELDS: 12 muffins

Source unknown

"Finger Licking Good Dressing"

Submitted by Debbie Cox
Richmond, Virginia

INGREDIENTS:

4 boxes of Stove Top Cornbread Dressing
¼ cup white raisins
½ cup Granny Smith apples, peeled
   and diced
1 medium or large onion, diced
1 green pepper or ½ cup

3 stems of celery, diced
¼ teaspoon Cayenne pepper
1 tablespoon garlic powder, or to taste
½ pound sage hot sausage
1 can chicken broth
⅓ teaspoon black pepper

Follow directions for Stove Top Stuffing Mix for 4 boxes. While mixture is boiling, mix in dry dressing with raisins, apples, cooked and drained sausage, celery, cayenne pepper, black pepper, onion, green pepper, and add in hot liquid mixture and mix well.

Stuff any turkey or fowl of your choice. The can of chicken broth is to be added as needed during mixing to assure the right moisture content that you prefer.

SERVES: 12 to 16

Original recipe

Challah

Submitted by Carol Jarett
Richmond, Virginia

INGREDIENTS:

2 packets dry yeast

⅓ cup sugar

1⅔ cups warm water (105°–115°), divided

¼ cup honey

½ cup vegetable oil

3 large eggs

2 teaspoons salt

7 to 7½ cups unbleached flour

Glaze:

1 egg yolk, beaten with 1 teaspoon water

In a large bowl, combine yeast with ⅔ cup of the water and 1 teaspoon of the sugar. Let mixture rest for 5 to 10 minutes, or until it begins to foam. Add the rest of the water, sugar, honey, oil, eggs, salt and 4 cups of flour. Beat with electric mixer for 3 minutes. By hand, or with heavy-duty mixer, slowly stir in enough of the remaining flour to form soft, slightly sticky dough. Cover with plastic wrap and let it rest for 5 minutes.

Turn dough out onto lightly floured surface and knead it for 10 minutes, adding small amounts of flour to keep it from sticking. Put dough into large oiled bowl and turn dough so all sides are oiled. Cover loosely with plastic wrap and then a dish towel. Let rise until doubled in bulk. This will take 1 to 2 hours, depending on room temperature.

Punch down dough, and knead a few times to remove air bubbles. Divide dough in half, cover loosely with plastic wrap, and let rest 10 minutes. Then form each piece, carefully, into a round loaf.

On lightly floured surface, roll the dough into a smooth 24″ long, even rope. Bring one end around into a circle about 5 inches in diameter. Continue winding rest of rope on top of circle so that it spirals inward and upward, finishing in the center. Tuck in end. Repeat for second loaf. Gently transfer each loaf to a greased 9″ cake pan. Lightly rub a little oil over surface of each loaf to keep it moist. Cover loosely with waxed paper, and let rise until double in size, 45 to 60 minutes. Brush loaves with the egg glaze, and bake them in a preheated 350° F oven for 40 to 45 minutes until crust is brown, and bottom sounds hollow when tapped. If loaves are browning too much, cover loosely with aluminum foil. Remove from pans, and cool on wire rack.

YIELDS: 2 large loaves

The Reflector Newspaper

Desserts and Sweets

Pineapple in Caramel Kirsch

Submitted by Annette Gelber
Richmond, Virginia

INGREDIENTS:

9 tablespoons butter

9 tablespoons sugar, divided

9 slices fresh pineapple, core removed

9 tablespoons Kirsch or other fruit brandy

9 scoops vanilla ice cream

Heat the butter in a skillet and add 3 tablespoons sugar. Add the pineapple rings and sprinkle with the remaining sugar. Cook 3 minutes on each side over moderate heat until the pineapple is golden brown and the sugar has carmelized. Heat the Kirsch in a small saucepan until hot but not boiling. Touch Kirsch with a match and carefully pour the flaming liquid over the pineapple. Serve hot with a scoop of ice cream.

This is a festive last minute dessert. Flame the kirsch at the table if you really want to show off!

SERVES: 9

Source unknown

Strawberries in Balsamic Vinegar

Submitted by Annette Gelber
Richmond, Virginia

INGREDIENTS:

1 pint strawberries
1 tablespoon sugar (or more to taste)
2 tablespoons good quality balsamic
    vinegar
Whipped cream for garnish (optional)

Purchased Amaretti cookies (found in
    high quality super-markets or Italian
    food stores)

Wash, hull and cut berries lengthwise. Toss with sugar and balsamic vinegar. Keep in refrigerator until ready to serve. Mix well and spoon berries and sauce into 4 pretty glass or crystal goblets. Serve with a dollop of whipped cream if desired.

This is a very simple dessert but quite elegant. Nice served with Amaretti cookies.

SERVES: 4

The Frugal Gourmet Cooks Italian

Strawberries in the Snow

Submitted by Becky McCann
Richmond, Virginia

INGREDIENTS:

2 quarts strawberries
¾ cup sugar
1 Angel Food Cake
4 ounces cream cheese, softened

½ cup sugar
1 pint whipping cream
2 teaspoons vanilla

Wash and slice berries and cover with ¾ cup sugar. Let sit at room temperature for at least 30 minutes until syrup forms, stirring often to help it along. Cube cake into bite size pieces and put in bottom of trifle dish or serving bowl. Using electric mixer, beat cream cheese and ½ cup sugar until creamy. Add whipping cream and vanilla and beat until stiff peaks form. Top cake with berries and berries with whipped cream. Cover with plastic wrap and refrigerate at least 4 hours before serving.

SERVES: 8–10

Family recipe

Blueberry Dessert

Submitted by Carolyn Cottrell
Wicomico Church, Virginia

INGREDIENTS:

1 6-ounce package black raspberry or
    black cherry Jello
2 cups boiling water

1 8¼-ounce can crushed pineapple
1 22-ounce can blueberry pie filling
1 cup chopped nuts

Dissolve Jello in boiling water. Add other ingredients. Chill in 11″ × 13″ pan.

TOPPING INGREDIENTS:

1 cup sour cream
½ cup sugar

6 ounces softened cream cheese
½ teaspoon vanilla

Beat together cream cheese and sugar. Add sour cream and vanilla. Spread on top.

SERVES: 12 to 15

Family recipe

Poached Pears in Ginger Syrup

Submitted by Stephanie Schonauer
Huntington Beach, California

INGREDIENTS:

2 cups water
⅔ cup sugar
7 quarter size slices fresh ginger

4 firm ripe, peeled pears (Bartlett or
Bosc), halved and cored

In a large stock pot, combine water, sugar and ginger. Bring to a boil and stir until sugar dissolves, about 2 minutes. Add pears and reduce heat to a lively simmer. Cook, basting occasionally, 15 minutes. Remove from heat and let pears cool in syrup 30 minutes. With slotted spoon, remove the pears from the liquid and place them in a bowl.

Boil the syrup briskly 2 minutes, or until it thickens. Pour it through a strainer onto the pears. Discard ginger. Chill fruit in its syrup until cold, about 2 hours. Serve in pretty bowls.

SERVES: 4

Source unknown

Any Fruit Cobbler

Submitted by Robbie Covington
Suffolk, Virginia

INGREDIENTS:

½ cup butter
2 quarts fruit
1½ cups sugar, divided

1 cup self-rising flour
1 cup milk

Put butter in bottom of 13×9×2 pan and melt. Add fruit with 1 cup sugar. Mix flour, milk and ½ cup sugar and pour over fruit. Bake 30 to 40 minutes in 350° F oven.

SERVES: 6 to 8

Family recipe

Best Black Cherry Compote

Submitted by Annette Gelber
Richmond, Virginia

INGREDIENTS:

1½ pounds ripe Bing cherries
1 cup granulated sugar
2 cups water
1 teaspoon vanilla

1 cup whipping cream
2 tablespoons powdered sugar
2–3 tablespoons Cointreau

Remove stems and pits from cherries.

Place sugar and water in a saucepan (medium size). Bring to a boil, stirring occasionally to help dissolve sugar. Remove from heat. Cool for exactly 5 minutes. Add vanilla, then place fruit in syrup and submerge. (Place over them a small bowl of raw rice sitting on a saucer.) Cool cherries in the syrup, then put in refrigerator until serving time. Whip cream with powdered sugar until thick but a bit runny. Add Cointreau. Reserve covered in refrigerator.

SERVES: 6

Jack Lirio's *Fast Fabulous Desserts*

Cherry Dessert

Submitted by Josephine Morris
Oliveburg, Pennsylvania

INGREDIENTS:

3 egg whites
½ teaspoon cream of tartar
1 cup sugar
1 cup soda crackers (crushed with hands)

½ cup nuts (chopped)
1 package Dream Whip
1 can Thank You Cherry Pie Filling

Beat egg whites and cream of tartar for 2 minutes. Fold in cup of sugar. Add crushed soda crackers and chopped nuts. Bake in 10 × 10″ greased pan for 25 minutes at 350° F. Let cool. Cover shell with Dream Whip. Spread can of cherry pie filling on top.

Note: Taken to church suppers. Easy, very good!

SERVES: 9 to 10

Family recipe

Holiday Fruit Compote

Submitted by Katie Hudson
Ruther Glen, Virginia

INGREDIENTS:

½ cup Port wine
2 tablespoons butter
2 cups sugar
1 tablespoon grated lemon peel
½ teaspoon ground cinnamon
¼ teaspoon ground nutmeg
¼ teaspoon ground cloves

4 medium apples, peeled and chopped
2 cups fresh cranberries
1 28-ounce can peaches, chopped
1 28-ounce can pears, chopped
1 cup chopped, pitted dates
½ cup chopped walnuts

In a slow-cooking pot, combine wine, butter, sugar, lemon peel, cinnamon, nutmeg, cloves, apples and cranberries. Cover and cook on low for 3 hours. Add peaches, pears, dates and nuts and cook an additional hour.

Serve warm or cold as a dessert or as a topping on vanilla ice cream.

SERVES: 12

Friend's recipe

Apricot Delight

Submitted by Deanie Mitchell
Richmond, Virginia

INGREDIENTS:

1 16-ounce can apricots, chopped and
    drained
1 16-ounce crushed pineapple, drained
2 cups cold water (part juice)

2 3-ounce apricot Jello
2 cups boiling water
2 large bananas, chopped
2 cups miniature marshmallows

Drain juice from fruit, (saving ½ cup of each for topping). Add juice to cold water to make 2 cups. Dissolve Jello in boiling water and mix with cold water. Stir and refrigerate until it starts to thicken. Mix Jello with apricot, pineapple, bananas and marshmallows. Place in 9 × 13 inch dish. Refrigerate until congealed.

TOPPING INGREDIENTS:

1 tablespoon butter
½ cup juice saved from apricots
½ cup juice saved from pineapple
1 egg

½ cup sugar
3 tablespoons flour
1 envelope Dream Whip (whipped)
½ cup mild grated cheddar cheese

Cook butter, juice from apricots and pineapple, egg, sugar and flour. Cook until thickened, stirring constantly. Let mixture cool; add grated cheese. Then stir in whipped Dream Whip. Spread on fruit Jello mixture.

SERVES: 16

Family recipe

Peach and Blueberry Crisp

Submitted by Jane Whitaker
Richmond, Virginia

TOPPING INGREDIENTS:

¾ cup packed brown sugar
¾ cup flour
½ cup unsalted butter, cut into pieces

1 cup old fashion oats
¾ cup chopped toasted pecans

Preheat oven to 350° F. Butter 9 × 13 glass baking dish.

Mix sugar and flour in medium bowl. Add butter and rub with fingertips until mixture resembles coarse crumbs. Mix in oats and pecans.

FRUIT INGREDIENTS:

6 tablespoons sugar
3 tablespoons flour
½ teaspoon cinnamon
⅛ teaspoon nutmeg

3½ pounds peaches, peeled, each cut into
6 wedges
1 pint blueberries

Mix sugar, flour, cinnamon and nutmeg in a large bowl. Add fruit and toss to coat. Transfer to baking dish. Sprinkle topping over it. Bake 45 minutes until topping is brown and filling bubbles. Serve with vanilla ice cream or frozen yogurt.

SERVES: 8

Bon Appetit Magazine (1992)

Blueberry Crisp

Submitted by Maureen Flattery
Midlothian, Virginia

INGREDIENTS:

1 pint blueberries (rinsed)
1 tablespoon lemon juice
½ cup brown sugar, firmly packed
½ cup all purpose flour

½ teaspoon ground cinnamon
½ teaspoon ground nutmeg
¼ cup butter or margarine (softened)
Vanilla ice cream, optional

Preheat oven to 375° F. Grease bottom of 8 × 8″ baking dish. Place blueberries in bottom. Sprinkle with lemon juice.

Mix together sugar, flour, cinnamon, nutmeg and butter or margarine until crumbly. Spread over blueberries. Bake 25 to 30 minutes. Serve warm with vanilla ice cream.

SERVES: 6

Family recipe

Oregon Blueberry Tart

Submitted by Pat Glupker
Richmond, Virginia

INGREDIENTS:

1 cup flour
2 tablespoons powdered sugar
½ cup butter
2 cups blueberries

1 10-ounce jar red currant jelly
¼ cup chopped walnuts
Whipped cream

Combine flour, powdered sugar and butter and press in 9″ tart pan. Bake at 425° F 10 to 12 minutes. Cool. Fill tart shell with blueberries. Heat the jelly until smooth and pour over the berries. Top with nuts. Chill. Serve topped with whipped cream.

SERVES: 8

Family recipe

Bread Pudding

Submitted by Mikki Jacques
Virginia Beach, Virginia

INGREDIENTS:

1 loaf (about 12 ounces) French bread, torn or cut into 1 or 2 inch pieces	1 teaspoon vanilla
⅓ cup raisins	1 cup granulated sugar
½ cup (unsalted) butter, melted	¾ cup brown sugar
2 cups heavy cream	1 teaspoon ground cinnamon
2 cups milk	1 teaspoon ground nutmeg
4 eggs	Orange Butter Sauce
	Whipped cream for garnish (optional)

Place bread pieces in a large (13 × 9 × 2) generously greased baking dish (pan). Sprinkle raisins over bread pieces. Drizzle melted butter over bread, mixing with hands to coat evenly.

In medium mixing bowl, beat cream, milk, eggs and vanilla. Add granulated sugar, brown sugar, cinnamon and nutmeg; blend well. Pour over mixture in pan. Let bread soak, pressing it gently to insure complete soaking, until there is little or no liquid in bottom of pan.

Put pan with bread mixture in a larger pan; fill pan with water half way up the sides of the bread filled pan. Bake in preheated 350° F oven for 45 to 60 minutes, or until well browned and risen as a soufflé.

Serve warm or at room temperature, accompanied by Orange Butter Sauce.

ORANGE BUTTER SAUCE INGREDIENTS:

¼ cup butter	4 tablespoons fresh orange juice
1½ cups granulated sugar	4 teaspoons orange rind
1 cup sour cream	

In medium saucepan, melt butter. Add sugar, sour cream, orange juice and rind. Bring to boil; cook, stirring constantly, until mixture is slightly thickened. Serve with Bread Pudding.

SERVES: 12

Source unknown

Blackberry Wine Cake

Submitted by Mary R. Lane
Hampton, Virginia

INGREDIENTS:

½ cup pecans, finely chopped
1 package white cake mix
1 package blackberry gelatin, preferably
  Royal brand gelatin (Winn-Dixie
  carries this brand of gelatin)
½ cup vegetable or canola oil
½ cup blackberry wine

4 large eggs
Glaze:
½ cup margarine or sweet butter, melted
  and cooled
½ blackberry wine
2 cups confectioners sugar, sifted

Preheat the oven to 350° F. Grease a 12-cup tube pan. Sprinkle the nuts evenly over the bottom of the pan. Set aside.

In a large mixing bowl, using an electric mixer, blend the cake mix, gelatin, oil, wine and eggs on low speed for one minute. Increase the speed to medium-high and beat for five minutes. Pour the batter into tube pan. Bake for 45 to 50 minutes, or until the top of the cake is brown and the sides have come away from the pan.

While the cake is baking, prepare the glaze in a medium-size mixing bowl. Combine the melted and cooled margarine and the wine. Gradually stir in the confectioner's sugar until the mixture is smooth

Remove the cake from the oven. With a fork, poke holes over the entire surface of the cake. Pour the glaze over the hot cake. Let cool in the pan for about an hour. Invert the glazed cake onto a plate and serve.

Note: Because I think the fork is too short and narrow, I use a long knitting needle to push holes into the surface of the cake. I also use a knife to separate the cake from the edges of the pan after baking.

SERVES: 18 (small slices)

Newspaper

Raw Apple Nut Cake

Submitted by Jane H. Settle-Stanley
Arlington, Virginia

INGREDIENTS:

1½ cups oil
2 cups sugar
3 eggs
2 teaspoons vanilla
3 cups flour
1 teaspoon salt
1 teaspoon soda

3 cups chopped apples
1 cup chopped nuts
Topping:
1 cup brown sugar
¼ cup milk
1 stick margarine

Mix oil, sugar, eggs, and vanilla. Sift dry ingredients of flour, salt, and soda together. Add to oil, sugar, eggs, and vanilla. Fold in chopped apples and nuts. Bake at 350° F for about one hour in a greased and floured bundt pan. Test with toothpick to determine when cake is done. Cool cake in pan for 10 to 15 minutes. Remove from pan and allow cake to cool to room temperature.

Topping: Combine brown sugar, milk, and margarine and cook in saucepan for 3 minutes. Punch holes in cake with toothpick. Drizzle topping over cake.

SERVES: 10 to 12

Original

Lemon Ice Box Cake

Submitted by Mary Morgan
Midlothian, Virginia

INGREDIENTS:

1½ 3-ounce packages Lemon Jello
    (=4½ ounces)
1 cup hot water
3 lemons, juice and grated rind
1 large can (12 ounces) evaporated milk,
    chilled 24 hours

1¼ cups sugar
1 angel food cake
½ cup whipping cream
12 orange sections

Combine Jello, water and lemon juice and rind. Chill until almost set. Whip evaporated milk and add sugar. Combine the two mixtures. Cut off brown from angel food cake and break cake into chunks bout the size of walnuts. Fold cake into lemon mixture. Put in tube or bundt pan and let set overnight in refrigerator. Whip cream and frost cake. Decorate with orange sections.

SERVES: 12

Family recipe

Best Pineapple Cake

Submitted by Clara Bray

CAKE INGREDIENTS:

1 20-ounce can crushed pineapple
   with juice
2 cups sugar
2 cups flour

2 eggs
1 teaspoon baking soda
1 teaspoon vanilla extract
1 cup chopped nuts

Preheat oven to 350° F. Mix all cake ingredients together and beat for 2 minutes. Bake in a greased 9″ × 13″ pan for 35 to 40 minutes. Frost while cake is still warm.

FROSTING INGREDIENTS:

1 8-ounce package cream cheese, softened
½ cup margarine

1 pound box powdered sugar
1 teaspoon vanilla extract

Beat all frosting ingredients together and spread on warm cake. Make frosting ahead. Has to "mellow" for 3 days.

SERVES: 12

Family recipe

Pineapple Upside Down Cake

Submitted by Karen Shea
Richmond, Virginia

INGREDIENTS:

⅓ cup butter
½ cup firmly packed dark brown sugar
1 (20-ounce) can sliced pineapple, drained

8 maraschino cherry halves, drained
14–16 pecan halves

CAKE INGREDIENTS:

1½ cups sifted flour
1 cup sugar
2 teaspoons baking powder
½ teaspoon salt
⅓ cup vegetable shortening

⅔ cup milk
1 teaspoon vanilla extract
½ teaspoon lemon extract
1 teaspoon finely grated lemon rind
1 egg

Preheat oven to 350° F. Melt butter in a heavy 10 inch skillet (cast iron is best, but if using skillet with wooden or plastic handle, wrap in heavy-duty foil to protect during baking) or 9 inch square baking pan.

Place butter in skillet to melt over low heat. Remove from burner and sprinkle brown sugar evenly over butter. Arrange pineapple slices over sugar. Fill spaces with cherries and pecans. Set aside.

Into a large mixer bowl, sift together flour, sugar, baking powder and salt. Add shortening and milk. Beat at lowest speed just to blend. Increase speed to medium and, scraping bowl and beaters once or twice, beat 2 minutes. Add vanilla and lemon extracts, lemon rind and egg. Beat 2 minutes longer. Pour batter evenly over pineapple layer. Bake until cake is golden brown and pulls from sides of skillet, 40 to 50 minutes. Cool upright on a wire rack for 3 to 4 minutes, loosen edges with the dull side of a knife blade and invert onto a heat-proof serving plate. Let stand 1 to 2 minutes before removing pan from top. Serve warm or cold with sweetened whipped cream.

SERVES: 16

Adapted from *The New Doubleday Cookbook*

Cheese Cake Italian

Submitted by Mikki Perri Jacques
Virginia Beach, Virginia

INGREDIENTS:

⅔ cup sugar
1 pound cream cheese
3 eggs (beaten)

½ teaspoon almond extract
1 graham cracker pie crust

Combine sugar, cream cheese, eggs and extract and beat until smooth. Pour into graham cracker crust (or well buttered 10″ inch pie plate). Bake at 350° F for 25 minutes. Remove from oven, and let cool for 20 minutes.

TOPPING INGREDIENTS:

1 pint sour cream
6 tablespoons sugar

2 teaspoons vanilla extract

Mix all ingredients to blend. Pour over top of pie and bake for another 10 to 20 minutes at 350° F. Cool and store in refrigerator.

SERVES: 12 to 15

Source unknown

Coconut Cream Cheese Pound Cake

Submitted by Tressie Smith
St. Albans, West Virginia

INGREDIENTS:

½ cup butter or margarine, softened
½ cup shortening
1 8-ounce package softened cream cheese
6 eggs

¼ teaspoon baking soda
1 teaspoon vanilla extract
1 6-ounce package frozen coconut, thawed
1 teaspoon coconut flavoring

Cream butter, shortening, and cream cheese; gradually add sugar, beating at medium speed of an electric mixer until light and fluffy. Add eggs, one at a time, beating after each addition. Combine flour, soda, and salt; add to creamed mixture, stirring just until blended. Stir in coconut and flavorings. Spoon batter into a greased and floured 10-inch tube pan; bake 350° F for 1 hour and 15 minutes, or until a wooden pick inserted in center comes out clean. Cool in pan, 10 to 15 minutes; remove from pan and cool completely.

YIELDS: 1 10-inch cake

Source unknown

Cherry Coffee Cake

Submitted by Winnie Ridill
Virginia Beach, Virginia

CRUMB MIX INGREDIENTS:

½ cup flour
¼ cup sugar

2 tablespoons soft margarine

CAKE MIX INGREDIENTS:

1½ cup flour
1 teaspoon baking powder
¼ teaspoon baking soda
½ teaspoon salt
½ cup sugar
½ cup milk

1 egg
1 teaspoon vanilla
½ cup minus 2 tablespoons margarine,
    softened
1 can cherry pie filling

Preheat oven to 350° F. Mix flour, sugar, and margarine in small bowl to make crumb mixture.

Mix cake mix in medium bowl in order of ingredients listed. Mix well. Grease (or Pam) a 9×13 (or 9×9) pan. Put cake batter in pan. Then add ½ the crumb mix. Then spread with cherry pie filling. Sprinkle with the other ½ of crumb mix. Bake 1 hour at 350° F.

SERVES: 12

Friend Tom

Sour Cream Coffee Cake

Submitted by Ann Bendheim
Richmond, Virginia

INGREDIENTS:

1 cup butter
2 cups plus 4 teaspoons sugar
2 eggs
1 cup sour cream
½ teaspoon vanilla

2 cups sifted flour
1 teaspoon baking powder
½ teaspoon salt
1 teaspoon cinnamon
1 cup chopped pecans

Cream butter with 2 cups sugar. Add eggs and beat well. Add sour cream and vanilla. Add sifted flour, baking powder and salt. Mix 4 teaspoons sugar, cinnamon and nuts. Put half of the batter in a greased 9 inch tube pan. Add ¾ of the nut mixture. Add remaining batter and then the remaining nut mixture on top. Bake at 350° F for 1 hour.

SERVES: 16

Family recipe

Ring Coffee Cake

Submitted by Babs Jackson,
President/CEO, HHH

INGREDIENTS:

1 cup sugar
1 cup butter
1 cup boiling water
3 eggs, beaten

2 cakes yeast, or 3 packages dry yeast,
   dissolved in 1 cup lukewarm water
6 cups unsifted flour
1 teaspoon salt

Cream sugar and butter together in a large bowl. Add boiling water, mix and cool. Add beaten eggs, mix. Add dissolved yeast, mix. Add flour, mixed with salt, a little at a time, mixing in well before adding more. Initially, mixture will be lumpy. Cover bowl with plastic wrap and refrigerate overnight to rise.

Divide dough (in thirds for three large coffee cakes baked on cookie sheets, or in fourths for four smaller cakes baked in 9" cake pans). Knead on a floured board (9 to 10 times).

Roll out each part into an oval/rectangle shape. Spread thinly with melted butter and sprinkle with a mixture of sugar and cinnamon. Sprinkle with raisins if desired. Roll up from the long side, then shape roll into a snail shape (crescent). Cover with greased wax paper and towels. Let rise for two hours. Bake in 350° F oven about 25 to 30 minutes.

FROSTING INGREDIENTS:

1 tablespoon butter
1 cup powdered sugar

1 tablespoon orange juice (may need more)

Blend butter with powdered sugar. Add tablespoon of orange juice and beat until smooth. Add a little bit more juice if necessary to make frosting a spreading consistency. Frost cakes and decorate with maraschino cherry halves and pecan halves.

SERVES: 8 to 10

Family recipe

Swiss Chocolate Cake

Submitted by Marian Sheffield
Blackstone, Virginia

CAKE INGREDIENTS:

1 box devil's food cake mix, 18.25 ounces
1 3½-ounce package vanilla instant
    pudding

1½ cups milk
3 eggs
1 cup vegetable oil

Preheat oven to 325° F. Combine cake mix with pudding mix, milk, eggs and oil. Grease 3 layer cake pans and pour in cake ingredients. Bake for 20 to 25 minutes. Check for doneness at 20 minutes.

ICING INGREDIENTS:

1 cup powdered sugar
1 package (8 ounces) cream cheese,
    softened

12 ounces Cool Whip
½ cup pecans, chopped
1 small Hershey Chocolate Bar, grated

Mix powdered sugar and cream cheese until smooth. Fold in Cool Whip and pecans. Stir in grated Hershey bar. Spread icing on cooled cake.

SERVES: 8

Adapted from Martha Grubb's recipe

Crazy Chocolate Cake

Submitted by Judy Nelson
Midlothian, Virginia

INGREDIENTS:

1½ cups cake flour
1 cup sugar
3 tablespoons cocoa
½ teaspoon salt
1 teaspoon soda

1 teaspoon vanilla extract
1 teaspoon distilled vinegar
5 tablespoons melted shortening or
    salad oil
1 cup water

Sift dry ingredients into ungreased cake pan (9″ round). Make 3 holes in the dry mixture. In the first hole pour the vanilla, in the second the vinegar and in the third the melted shortening or oil. Then pour the water over the entire mixture and mix thoroughly. Bake 30 minutes at 350° F in same pan. Ice when cool in same pan.

BUTTER ICING INGREDIENTS:

½ pound powdered sugar
¼ stick of butter, softened

½ teaspoon vanilla
1½–2 tablespoons milk

In medium bowl, beat together all ingredients until smooth. If necessary, add more milk until frosting will spread easily.

SERVES: 6 to 8

Family recipe

Mississippi Mud Cake

Submitted by Marion Badenock
Reedville, Virginia

CAKE INGREDIENTS:

1 cup margarine, softened
2 cups sugar
4 eggs
1½ cups sifted flour

1 cup coconut
1½ cups chopped pecans
1 teaspoon vanilla extract

Cream margarine and sugar together, add remaining cake ingredients. Bake in greased 13″×9″ pan at 350° F for 40 minutes. While cake is still hot, spread with mini-marshmallows and cover tightly with lid. (This ingredient listed under "Topping".)

TOPPING INGREDIENTS:

2 cups mini-marshmallows
1 pound powdered sugar, sifted
¼ cup milk

½ cup margarine, softened
½ cup cocoa
1 teaspoon vanilla extract

Beat sugar, milk, margarine, cocoa and vanilla. When cake is cool, spread with topping.

SERVES: 15

Family recipe

Easy Chocolate Chess Pie

Submitted by Evelyn P. Foster
Prince George, Virginia

INGREDIENTS:

2½ cups sugar
4 eggs
1 tablespoon vanilla
7 tablespoons cocoa

1½ cups evaporated milk (12-ounce can)
1 stick butter, melted
2 8-inch frozen pie crusts

Preheat oven to 350° F.

Put sugar, eggs, vanilla, cocoa, milk, and butter in blender and mix well. Pour into pie shells and bake 35 to 40 minutes or until top of pie has puffed up like a souffle. The center will be shaky when pie is taken from the oven. Do not overbake. Serve with whipped topping for a special treat.

SERVES: 8

Source unknown (original)

Cantaloupe Pie

Submitted by Joyce Fleet
Mechanicsville, Virginia

INGREDIENTS:

1 cup sugar
2 tablespoons flour
3 eggs, beaten
1 cup pureed cantaloupe

1 teaspoon vanilla
2 tablespoons butter (or margarine)
1 baked 8″ pastry shell
1 cup whipped cream

Combine sugar and flour in a saucepan, add eggs mixing well. Stir in cantaloupe puree. Cook over medium heat 8 to 10 minutes until mixture boils and thickens. Remove from heat and stir in vanilla and butter. Cool.

Pour mixture into pie shell and spread evenly with whipped cream. Chill, slice and serve.

SERVES: 6

Original recipe

Gingersnap Pumpkin Pie

Submitted by Kathy Markel
Richmond, Virginia

INGREDIENTS:

1¾ cups gingersnap crumbs (about 43
   cookies, finely crushed)
2½ tablespoons reduced-calorie stick
   margarine, melted
2 tablespoons granulated sugar
Cooking spray
1½ cups fresh or canned pumpkin puree
¾ cup packed brown sugar

1 tablespoon cornstarch
1 teaspoon ground cinnamon
1 teaspoon vanilla extract
¼ teaspoon salt
¼ teaspoon ground nutmeg
2 large egg whites
1 large egg
1 (12-ounce) can evaporated skim milk

Preheat oven to 325° F. Combine gingersnap crumbs, margarine and sugar in a bowl; toss with a fork until moist. Press into bottom and up sides of a 9-inch pie plate coated with cooking spray. Bake at 325° F for 5 minutes; cool on a wire rack. Combine pumpkin and remaining ingredients in a bowl. Pour into prepared crust. Bake at 325° F for 1 hour or until a knife inserted in center comes out clean. Cool on a wire rack.

SERVES: 6

Family recipe

Pumpkin Ice Cream Pie

Submitted by Cheryll Nachman
Midlothian, Virginia

INGREDIENTS:

1 8-ounce can (or one cooked and
   mashed) pumpkin
½ cup firmly packed brown sugar
¼ teaspoon ground nutmeg
½ teaspoon ground cinnamon

1 quart softened vanilla ice cream
1 9" inch graham cracker crust
1 cup whipped cream
Chopped pecans to garnish

Combine pumpkin, sugar, cinnamon, and nutmeg in a large mixing bowl, stirring until sugar dissolves. Add ice cream and mix thoroughly. Spoon into graham cracker crust; freeze for at least 8 hours. Garnish with whipped cream and chopped pecans. Let stand at room temperature for 5 minutes before serving.

SERVES: 6 to 8

Toasted Coconut Pie

Submitted by Grace W. Bailey
Richmond, Virginia

INGREDIENTS:

3 beaten eggs
1½ cups sugar
½ cup butter or margarine, melted
4 teaspoons lemon juice

1 teaspoon vanilla
1⅓ cups flaked coconut
1 9" unbaked pie shell

Thoroughly combine eggs, sugar, butter or margarine, lemon juice and vanilla; stir in coconut. Pour filling into 9" unbaked pie shell. Bake in moderate oven 350° F for 40 to 45 minutes, or till knife inserted half-way between center and edge comes out clean. Cool before serving.

SERVES: 6 to 8

Better Homes & Gardens Magazine

Great Fruit Pie/Cobbler

Submitted by Sue Garber Stewart
Richmond, Virginia

INGREDIENTS:

1 cup sugar
1 cup flour
1 cup milk

1 stick butter (4 ounces)
3 teaspoons baking powder
1 quart fruit, heated and sweetened to taste

Preheat oven to 370° F. Melt butter in 9 × 13 glass pan in the oven while preheating. Stir together sugar, flour, baking powder and milk. Pour over melted butter in dish. Carefully pour heated fruit over batter. Bake for approximately 25 minutes or until golden brown on top. Serve with whipped cream or ice cream.

SERVES: 8 to 10

Source unknown

Amish Butterscotch Pie

Submitted by Sue Garber Stewart
Richmond, Virginia

INGREDIENTS:

1 cup brown sugar, firmly packed
1¼ cups milk
2 tablespoons butter
2 eggs
½ cup sugar

1 tablespoon all-purpose flour
¼ teaspoon salt
1 teaspoon vanilla extract
1 baked 9-inch pie shell

Combine all the ingredients (with exception of the pie shell) in a blender and blend well. Cook over low heat in a saucepan until thickened. Pour mixture into the baked pie shell and bake for 8 minutes at 400° F, being careful not to brown the top.

Top with whipped cream or meringue.

SERVES: 8

Source unknown

Gertrude's Rhubarb Pie

Submitted by Elizabeth Hopper
Richmond, Virginia

INGREDIENTS:

3 cups sliced rhubarb
1 cup white sugar
3 tablespoons flour

½ teaspoon nutmeg
2 beaten eggs or ½ cup egg substitute
1 9″ pie shell, unbaked

Preheat oven to 450° F. Combine Rhubarb, sugar, flour and nutmeg in bowl. Mix in eggs. Pour into unbaked pie shell. Bake at 450° F for 10 minutes. Lower heat to 350° F for approximately 30 minutes or until knife comes out clean. Good warm or cold.

SERVES: 6

Family recipe

Peter Peter Pumpkin Mousse

Submitted by Jeannine Daniel
Midlothian, Virginia

INGREDIENTS:

1 4-ounce package butterscotch instant
   pudding and pie filling
1 4-ounce package vanilla instant pudding
   and pie filling
2½ cups cold milk

2 cups canned pumpkin
½ teaspoon each: ground cinnamon,
   nutmeg and ginger
2 cups thawed Cool Whip

Combine puddings, milk, pumpkin and spices, then beat. Fold in Cool Whip. To serve, top with whipped cream and candy corn.

Note: Children love to make this for Christmas and Thanksgiving.

SERVES: 8

Source unknown

Cappuccino Parfait

Submitted by Fran Gregory
Richmond, Virginia

INGREDIENTS:

½ teaspoon ground cinnamon
1 teaspoon grated orange rind
1½ cups of butterscotch sauce

½ gallon of coffee ice cream
Whipped cream and additional grated
   orange rind

Mix cinnamon, orange rind and butterscotch sauce in a bowl. Layer this alternately with coffee ice cream in parfait glasses. Place in the freezer until serving time. At serving, top with whipped cream and grated orange rind.

SERVES: 10 to 12

Source unknown

Orange Ruddian Cream

Submitted by Annette Gelber
Richmond, Virginia

INGREDIENTS:

¾ cup sugar

1 envelope unflavored gelatin

1 teaspoon grated orange peel

2 cups whipping cream, divided

1½ cups vanilla or plain yogurt

1 teaspoon vanilla

2 tablespoons grated semi-sweet chocolate

Optional garnish: candied orange peel

In a 1½ to 2 quart pan, mix sugar and gelatin. Add ½ cup water and orange peel; stir over high heat until boiling (about 2 minutes).

Remove from heat, add 1 cup cream which has not been whipped, yogurt and vanilla. Whisk to blend smoothly. Pour into ramekins or custard cups (6 ounce size). Chill until firm, at least 3 hours; cover airtight if storing up to 1 day.

Uncover desserts and sprinkle equally with grated chocolate. Whip remaining 1 cup of cream and top each dessert with a good portion of same. Optional: arrange a few orange strips atop cream.

CANDIED ORANGE PEEL INGREDIENTS:

2 medium size oranges

2 cups water

½ cup sugar

½ cup water

Using a zester (a hand tool with metal head having five small holes at one end) scrape down the 2 oranges to get long shreds of peel. Be careful not to scrape the white pith from underneath the peel as it is bitter.

Boil the 2 cups of water and place peel in same. Turn down heat and simmer the peel for 5 minutes. Drain, rinse once or twice, then drain again. Bring ½ cup sugar plus ½ cup water to a boil in small saucepan, stirring occasionally to dissolve sugar. Place drained peel in the hot syrup; remove from heat and allow to cool. Store peel in syrup in refrigerator. At serving time, remove peel from syrup with a fork, placing small mounds on top of whipped cream. Any remaining peel can be replaced in the syrup and stored again in refrigerator where it will keep for a couple of weeks.

SERVES: 6

Friend

Caramel Icing

Submitted by Bonnie Foster
Prince George, Virginia

INGREDIENTS:

1 stick butter
1 cup brown sugar, packed

¼ cup milk
2½ cups confectioners sugar

Cook brown sugar and butter for 2 minutes, add milk and boil 2 minutes longer. Cool. Add 2½ cups confectioners sugar and beat until smooth.

YIELDS: Icing for one cake

Family recipe

Hot Fudge Sauce

Submitted by Annette Gelber
Richmond, Virginia

INGREDIENTS:

½ cup cornstarch
1 cup sugar
1 pint dark corn syrup
1 cup milk
1½ packages (4 ounces each) sweet
    chocolate, broken

5 squares (1 ounce each) unsweetened
    chocolate, broken
¼ cup butter
1 teaspoon vanilla extract

Combine cornstarch and sugar in large, heavy saucepan. Stir in corn syrup, then milk. Add 1½ packages sweet broken chocolate and the 5 squares (1 ounce each) unsweetened chocolate, broken; heat to boiling, stirring occasionally until chocolate is melted. Reduce heat to simmer; cook until sauce is glossy, about 1½ minutes. Remove from heat; stir in butter and vanilla and cool. Serve over your choice of ice cream, plain pound cake or angel food cake.

Note: This is the best hot fudge sauce recipe I have ever made. Leftover sauce can be refrigerated for a week or frozen if it is to be kept for a longer period of time. In either case, be sure to bring it to room temperature before re-heating on low; stir occasionally to ensure that sauce does not stick to pan.

SERVES: Approximately 1½ pints

Original recipe

Chocolate Chip Cookies

Submitted by Kathie Markel
Richmond, Virginia

INGREDIENTS:

2 cups flour
1½ cups oatmeal, chopped in food processor
½ teaspoon salt
½ teaspoon baking powder
1 teaspoon baking soda
1 cup real butter, softened
1 cup granulated sugar

1 cup brown sugar
2 eggs
2 teaspoons vanilla
2 cups (12 ounce) chocolate chips (extra appreciated)
1½ cups nuts, chopped (optional)

Mix flour, chopped oatmeal, salt, baking powder and baking soda in a bowl. Set aside. Cream butter with mixer, add sugars and blend. Add eggs and vanilla. Slowly add flour mixture and beat till well blended. Stir in chocolate chips and nuts by hand. Preheat oven to 375° F. Bake cookies 11 minutes or until just browned (oven dependent).

YIELDS: 5 dozen cookies

Original recipe

Ukrainian Holiday Cookies

Submitted by Grace Cibula
Hopewell, Virginia

INGREDIENTS:

1 cup (2 sticks) butter or margarine, softened
½ cup sugar
1 egg white
1 teaspoon vanilla extract

2 cups flour
2 cups walnuts, hazelnuts, or pecans, chopped
1 cup powdered sugar
1 teaspoon salt

Cream butter until soft. Add sugar, salt, and egg white; mix well. Add vanilla. Gradually add flour to creamed mixture. Add nuts to mixture. Roll dough into one-inch diameter balls. Arrange on lightly greased baking sheet; bake for 12 minutes at 350° F. Sift powdered sugar into shallow dish. Roll hot cookies in sugar until evenly coated. Cool on wire rack.

YIELDS: 3 to 4 dozen cookies

Family recipe

Great Pumpkin Cookies

Submitted by Kathy Burns
Richmond, Virginia

INGREDIENTS:

2 cups all purpose flour
1 cup oatmeal (uncooked, instant or old
    fashion)
1 teaspoon baking soda
2 teaspoons ground cinnamon
½ teaspoon salt
1 cup butter, softened
1 cup brown sugar, firmly packed

1 cup sugar
1–2 eggs slightly beaten (depending
    on size)
1½ teaspoons vanilla extract
1½ cups solid packed pumpkin
1 cup semi sweet chocolate morsels
1 cup raisins

Preheat oven at 350° F. Combine flour, oatmeal, baking soda, cinnamon, and salt. Cream butter and sugars until light and fluffy. Add eggs and vanilla to butter mixture. Alternate adding dry mixture and pumpkin to butter mixture, mixing well. Stir in chocolate morsels and raisins. On greased cookie sheet put ¼ cup dough for each cookie. If desired, can be shaped into pumpkins with stems on top. Bake 20 to 25 minutes or until slightly firm and lightly brown.

Can be topped with icing, raisins, candy pieces, etc. (If using icing, wait until cookies are cooled.)

YIELDS: 2 dozen

Original recipe

Pecan Delights

Submitted by Teresa Banyas
Clarksville, Virginia

INGREDIENTS:

1 cup butter
½ cup sugar
1 tablespoon water

1 teaspoon vanilla extract
2 cups all purpose flour
2 cups chopped pecans

Cream butter; gradually blend in sugar. Stir in water and vanilla. Combine flour and nuts and; add to creamed mixture. With lightly floured hands, mold cookies in shape of dates and put on ungreased cookie sheets. Bake at 325° F for 25 to 30 minutes or until light brown. Roll in granulated sugar while still warm.

YIELDS: about 5 dozen cookies

Source unknown

Real Scotch Shortbread

Submitted by Mildred P. Daffron
Chester, Virginia

INGREDIENTS:

1 pound butter, softened (no substitutions)
½ cup sugar
2 tablespoons cornstarch
2 cups all-purpose flour

Few drops lemon extract (can use vanilla
  or almond extract if preferred)
Powdered sugar, optional

Do all mixing by hand. Cream butter and sugar; gradually, add cornstarch mixed with flour, then flavorings. Pat into 3 circles, each about 6 inches in diameter and ¼ inch thick. Place on ungreased cookie sheet. Pierce each circle with fork. Bake at 325° F for 20 to 25 minutes, until lightly browned at edge. (Optional: sprinkle with powdered sugar when done.) Cool slightly and cut into squares; remove from pan when completely cooled. Check frequently while cooking. They burn easily.

YIELDS: 24 Pieces

Family recipe

Crumb Cookies

Submitted by Bea Goldberg
Richmond, Virginia

INGREDIENTS:

½ cup butter
½ cup margarine
¾ cup sugar

2½ cups all purpose flour
Ground cinnamon to taste

Process all ingredients as for crumbs in crumb cake. (Pulse in processor, or combine all and cut into crumbs with 2 knives.) Pat onto cookie sheet. Bake at 350° F about 15 to 20 minutes. Remove from oven and cut immediately. (I use pizza cutter.) Let stand as is until cool and crisp (about 1 hour). Separate with spatula and move to storage container.

Note: Does not need refrigeration and lasts indefinitely. Simple and delicious!

YIELDS: about 60 cookies

Family recipe

Buckeyes

Submitted by Marjorie Hephner
Midlothian, Virginia

INGREDIENTS:

1 pound butter, softened
2 pounds peanut butter
3 pounds powdered sugar

2 (12 ounce) packages semi-sweet
chocolate morsels
4 squares (1 ounce each) unsweetened
chocolate

Beat together butter, peanut butter and powdered sugar. Form into small balls (bite size), and freeze. Melt together chocolate morsels and unsweetened chocolate in double boiler. Dip frozen balls in chocolate mixture (using a toothpick) until almost covered. Make it look like an Ohio Buckeye. Place on a waxed paper covered cookie sheet. Freeze for 1 hour and then store in a plastic bag.

Variation: An alternative chocolate dip would be 2 (12 ounce) packages of chocolate morsels and ½ cake paraffin melted in double boiler.

YIELDS: 200 buckeyes

Family recipe

Brownies

Submitted by Barbara S. Walser

INGREDIENTS:

1 cup butter (do not substitute)
4 (1-ounce) squares unsweetened
chocolate
4 eggs
2 cups sugar

1 cup flour
1 cup walnuts, finely chopped
2 teaspoons vanilla extract
Dash salt

Preheat oven to 325° F. Melt butter and chocolate together; cool. Beat eggs well; add sugar. Add to chocolate mixture; stir in flour and vanilla. Fold in chopped nuts. Mix well.

Grease a 9×13×2 glass pan. Pour batter into pan and bake 40 minutes. Cool about 15 minutes. Cut into bite size pieces. Cool in glass pan.

YIELDS: about 40 bite-size brownies

Family recipe

Oatmeal Chocolate Chip Bars

Submitted by Eunice Kay
Mechanicsville, Virginia

INGREDIENTS:

1½ cups firmly packed brown sugar
1 cup margarine
2 tablespoons molasses
2 teaspoons vanilla extract
2 eggs
3 cups quick-cooking rolled oats

1 cup all purpose flour
1 teaspoon baking soda
1 teaspoon salt
1 (12 ounce) package semi-sweet
    chocolate morsels
¾ cup chopped nuts

Heat oven to 350° F. Grease 13×9-inch pan. Combine sugar and margarine; beat until fluffy. Add molasses, vanilla and eggs; blend well. Stir in oats, flour, baking soda and salt. Beat well. Stir in nuts and chocolate morsels. (Batter will be stiff). Spread in pan. Bake 20 to 25 minutes until light golden brown and center is set. Cool slightly. Cut into bars.

YIELDS: 24

Family recipe

Chocolate Chip Cheese Bars

Submitted by Charlotte Hayman
Reedville, Virginia

INGREDIENTS:

1 tube (18 ounce) refrigerated chocolate
    chip cookie dough
1 package (8 ounce) cream cheese,
    softened

½ cup sugar
1 egg

Cut cookie dough in half. Press half the dough in bottom of greased 8 inch square baking dish. Beat cream cheese, sugar and egg until smooth. Spread over crust. Crumble remaining dough over the top. Bake at 350° F for 35 to 40 minutes. Cool on wire rack. Refrigerate leftovers.

SERVES: 12 to 16

Family recipe

Lemon Bars

Submitted by Annette Gelber
Richmond, Virginia

INGREDIENTS:

½ cup powdered sugar
1½ cups flour
½ teaspoon salt

¾ cup (1½ sticks) unsalted butter (cut in
    small pieces)

TOPPING:

4 eggs
1½ cups granulated sugar
Grated rind of 1 large lemon

½ cup fresh lemon juice
¼ cup whipping cream
Confectioners' sugar to dust

Preheat oven to 325° F. Grease 9″ × 13″ baking pan.

Sift sugar, flour and salt into a bowl. With a pastry blender, cut in the butter until the mixture resembles coarse crumbs. Press mixture into the bottom of the prepared pan and bake until golden brown, about 20 to 25 minutes.

Meanwhile, for the topping, whisk the eggs and sugar until blended. Add the lemon rind and juice and mix well. Lightly whip the cream and fold into the egg mixture. Pour over the still warm crust, return to the oven and bake until set, about 40 minutes.

Cool completely before cutting into bars. Dust with confectioners' sugar.

YIELDS: about 32 bars

Adapted from *Baking* by Carole Clements

Easy Turtle Bars

Submitted by Willoughby Adams
Richmond, Virginia

INGREDIENTS:

2 cups graham cracker crumbs
½ cup butter, melted
2 cups semi-sweet chocolate morsels

1 cup chopped nuts (peanuts, pecans or
    walnuts)
1 small jar caramel ice cream topping

Combine butter and graham crackers and press into a 13 × 9 pan. Sprinkle chocolate morsels and nuts on top. Remove lid from caramel topping, heat for 1 to 1½ minutes on high in microwave. Stir and drizzle over morsels and nuts. Bake at 300° F for 15 minutes. Chill thoroughly before cutting into 36 bars.

YIELDS: 36 bars

Rolled Baklava

Submitted by Maria Romhilt
Richmond, Virginia

INGREDIENTS:

3½ cups chopped walnuts	1¼ cups unsalted butter, melted
6 tablespoons sugar	1 pound box phyllo pastry sheets
2 teaspoons ground cinnamon	

Mix nuts, sugar, and cinnamon together. Melt butter and discard solids at bottom of pan. Take 1 pastry sheet and brush entire surface with butter. Add 2 more sheets and brush with butter between each sheet. Sprinkle with about ⅓ cup of nut mixture. Add 2 more sheets, brushing with butter and sprinkle with ⅓ cup of nuts. Repeat with 2 more sheets and sprinkle with ⅓ cup nuts. Roll up lengthwise to form a roll. Place seam side down and brush with butter. Cut into 1″ slices and place on baking sheet. Bake at 325° F for about 20 minutes. Cool and soak well with syrup.

SYRUP INGREDIENTS:

3 cups sugar	8–10 whole cloves
2 cups water	Juice of 1 lemon plus rind cut into pieces
1 stick cinnamon	⅓ cup honey

Boil sugar, water, cinnamon, cloves, and lemon juice and rind for 10 to 15 minutes. Add honey and boil for 2 more minutes.

Pour hot syrup over cool pastry. Let pastries soak in syrup for 45 to 60 minutes, turning over once during that time. Place each pastry in a cupcake liner and store in freezer.

YIELDS: 3 dozen

Family recipe

Index

Salads, Dressings, and Condiments

Eggs and Cheese

Entrees

Pasta and Rice

Equivalents

Will a 5-pound bag contain enough flour for those bread recipes you only bake once a year for holiday gifts? How many fresh lemons should you squeeze for 3 tablespoons of juice? And if you need 3 cups of cubed chicken for a brunch salad, how much chicken should you cook? Use this chart to eliminate the guesswork!

Ingredient	Equivalent
Dry Goods	
4 cups all-purpose flour	1 pound
2 cups granulated sugar	1 pound
4 to 4-1/2 cups confectioners' sugar	1 pound
2-1/4 cups brown sugar	1 pound
5-1/3 cups rolled oats	1 pound
3 to 4 cups cooked rice	1 cup uncooked long-grain rice
2 cups cooked rice	1 cup quick-cooking rice
2-1/4 cups cooked macaroni	1 cup (4 ounces) uncooked macaroni
2 cups cooked noodles	4 ounces uncooked noodles
4 cups cooked spaghetti	7 ounces uncooked spaghetti
6 cups cooked beans	1 pound dry beans (2-1/2 cups)
Crumbs	
1 cup soft bread crumbs	2 slices fresh bread
1 cup gingersnap crumbs	14 cookies
1 cup vanilla wafer crumbs	26-30 cookies
1 cup graham cracker crumbs	11-12 squares (1/4 pound)
1/2 cup pretzel crumbs	12 thin pretzels
Dairy	
1 cup egg whites	Whites of 6 to 7 large eggs
1 cup egg yolks	Yolks of 11-12 large eggs
2 cups whipped cream	1 cup (1/2 pint) heavy cream
2 cups butter or margarine	1 pound
1 cup shredded cheese	4 ounces cheese
1 cup cream or cottage cheese	8 ounces
1 cup grated Parmesan	3 ounces
Flavorings	
2 to 4 tablespoons lemon juice and 1 teaspoon grated peel (colored part only)	1 lemon
6 to 8 tablespoons orange juice and 2 to 3 tablespoons grated peel (colored part only)	1 orange
1 cup chocolate chips	6 ounces
1 square unsweetened chocolate	1 ounce
2 cups cocoa	8 ounces